EAT UP!

the healthy weight gain cookbook

lee gold

Lothian
BOOKS

Thomas C. Lothian Pty Ltd
132 Albert Road, South Melbourne 3205
www.lothian.com.au

National Library of Australia
Cataloguing-in-Publication data:

Gold, Lee.

   Eat up! : the healthy weight gain cookbook.

   ISBN 0 7344 0395 X.

   1. Weight gain. 2. Cookery. I. Title.

641.563

Design by Elizabeth Dias
Cover photograph by Jimmy Pozarik
Typeset by Grand Graphix Pty Ltd, Melbourne
Printed in Singapore by SNP SPrint Pte Ltd

Disclaimer

The author has made every effort to ensure that the information and advice in
this book is complete and accurate. However, the information, ideas, suggestions
and dietary advice contained in this book are not intended as a substitute for
consulting your doctor and obtaining medical supervision regarding any action
that may affect your well-being. Individual readers must assume responsibility for
their own actions, safety and health. Neither the author nor the publisher shall
be liable or responsible for any loss, injury, or damage allegedly arising from any
information or suggestion in this book.

Contents

foods individually so that they are identifiable. Making food tasty is important, particularly with the elderly. They often lose their senses of taste and smell, so food becomes less appealing overall and is even more so when puréed. To maximise swallowing and nutrition look at enhancing flavours through the use of spices, sauces, gravy, chutneys and salt.'

Monika is quick to dispel the myth that liquids are the easiest to swallow. 'For some people drinking is the hardest action of all because they cannot control fluids in their mouth,' she said. 'Even purées can be difficult for those with poor tongue movement. Sometimes thickened fluids are the safest and easiest to swallow. However, straws are only useful if the person is capable of sufficient suction.'

Of perhaps greater importance is the moisture content of food. 'A person with a weak tongue or a dry mouth finds it more difficult to swallow dry food,' Monika said. An excessively dry mouth can be relieved by sipping cold water or sucking ice cubes, taking lemon drinks or using artificial saliva stimulants.

Monika said carers need also to understand that the temperature of food and drink can influence the way it is perceived and accepted by the mouth. Dishes served at room temperature, for example, are commonly viewed as less palatable than slightly warmer or cooler meals. Similarly, slightly chilled water is often more tempting than that served at room temperature.

'Altering the temperature of food or drink can give a person greater control of it in their mouth and make swallowing easier,' Monika said. 'It's also important for the diner to feel comfortable when they are eating and not to be rushed.'

BASIC TIPS TO AID SWALLOWING

- Prepare soft-textured, moist foods.
- Choose ripe fruit and vegetables and tender cuts of meat, which are best steamed or casseroled.
- Keep the person's mouth moist by offering fluids throughout the day. The elderly, in particular, rarely drink enough. It may help the person to take smaller sips and to slow down the rate of fluid intake.
- Add moisture to food using gravies, creams, sauces, etc.
- Avoid giving caffeine and alcohol – these act as diuretics and may cause dehydration.
- Keep the mouth clean and maintain good oral care.

3 Strategies for gaining weight

Gaining weight in a healthy fashion demands a conscious commitment to combine good nutrition, regular exercise and stress-management techniques. Small changes to our diet and lifestyle can add up to major changes in overall health and well-being. It's all within our grasp.

We each have our personal nutritional needs, depending on our eating habits, energy requirements, exercise routine, health and medication schedule. By getting in touch with the rhythms of our bodies we can determine what is causing us to lose weight. People with more complex complaints may need professional support, but you can embark on the quest to gain weight by following a few simple steps.

The first step involves assessing what you eat and learning what foods deliver the most calories – the amount of energy released when the food is burned. It is not enough to eat more or more often; the precise food we choose influences how much weight we gain. A nutritious diet, rich in calories and containing a balance of carbohydrates, proteins, vitamins and minerals, is the perfect start.

Secondly, you need to consider how you feel about food and the conditions under which you usually eat. Have you started viewing food as 'good' or 'bad'? Do you grab meals on the run or eat in front of the television? Ideally, eating should be an enjoyable, social event and food seen as the fuel we need to nourish ourselves physically and psychologically. Removing negative associations about food and reducing other stresses in our lives will help us rediscover the pleasure of eating.

A nutritious diet

A nutritious diet supplies the body with all the nutrients it needs, including protein, carbohydrate, fat, fibre, vitamins and minerals, and water. You can help maintain a healthy body and mind by eating a variety of foods each day from the five main food groups – breads and cereals; fruit and vegetables; meat and meat alternatives; milk and dairy foods; butter, margarine and oils.

As a guide, each day we should aim to consume at least six servings of breads and cereals; 2–3 pieces of fruit and four servings of vegetables; 1–2 servings of meat or meat alternatives (like legumes and pulses), fish and eggs; 450 millilitres of milk or dairy foods for adults (and 600–900 millilitres for children and adolescents) and just 3–6 teaspoons of butter, margarine and oils.

Complex carbohydrates – found in breads, cereals, rice, pasta and some vegetables - are the body's main source of energy and should make up the bulk of our diet. Limit your consumption of simple carbohydrates like sugar, honey, molasses and fruit juice.

Protein is essential for keeping the immune system strong, helping our body to resist infection and for the growth and repair of new cells and tissue, including muscle. Protein-rich foods also supply vitamins and minerals, particularly iron and zinc. Fish, for example, contains the oil omega-3 that can be beneficial to the heart, circulation and the immune system. Increasing the amount of protein in your diet is often an effective way of increasing your energy levels, but should only be done if you are free from kidney or liver problems.

Try to include complex carbohydrates and proteins in each meal or snack. Foods like rice, pasta, grains, bread and breakfast cereals not only contain carbohydrates but also protein, fibre, vitamins and minerals. Wholemeal or wholegrain types are preferable to white varieties, as they contain more vitamins, minerals and fibre.

The advantages of a healthy diet are numerous. Eating well keeps us strong, helps us fight infection, slows or prevents the breakdown of body tissues, improves our emotional state, boosts our energy levels, improves our body's ability to cope with medical treatments and helps maximise the effectiveness of drug treatments.

Making calories count

Meeting basic nutritional and energy requirements is rarely enough for those people keen to restore lost weight. On top of maintaining a healthy weight you will need to build extra lean body mass and that involves consuming more calories than you burn. The best way to begin is to increase the amount of complex carbohydrates, starches and proteins, and lastly fats, in your diet. It's not only good for you; adding more calories to each mouthful can become a creative and flavoursome experience.

The calorie content of food is the amount of carbohydrates, proteins and fats it contains. Some foods are higher in calories than others – namely bread, cereal, rice and pasta; fruits (canned and dried); avocados, potatoes, peas, corn; meat, poultry, fish, dried beans, eggs and nuts; milk, fruited yoghurts, hard cheeses, ice-cream, custards and milk shakes.

Fats – commonly eaten in the form of butter, margarine, oil and cream – are very high in energy and can add calories without increasing the amount of food we eat, which is useful for people with small appetites. They also help maintain healthy skin and hair, protect our organs, help transport fat-soluble vitamins, and provide a reserve fuel supply. But excess fat in our diet tends to be stored as body fat rather than muscle and may increase the risk of heart disease and raise cholesterol levels. It can also worsen some forms of diarrhoea, so should be taken only in moderation.

Eating a carbohydrate-rich snack or meal that also contains moderate protein within two hours of completing a workout may help you to optimise gains in muscle mass, by promoting the production of natural anabolic hormones and supplying amino acids for protein synthesis. If you're weight training it may be even more effective to consume this snack before your workout. The Australian Institute of Sport encourages athletes to consume a snack providing 1 gram of carbohydrate per kilogram of body weight plus 7–10 grams of protein within 30 minutes of completing training. Some athletes also find that increasing their protein intake the day after a workout, during the recovery period, can boost weight gain.

FIRST-HAND: BULKING UP

Fitness consultant and former chef Nathan Tamihana, 28, has ambitions of playing first-grade rugby union and competing in a natural body-building competition.

'I can eat all day, every day, and not put on weight,' said Nathan. 'I have the biggest appetite but I'm finding it very hard to put on bulk.'

Nathan tips the scales at 75 kilograms but his ideal weight is more like 85 kilograms. A natural athlete, he enjoys playing rugby and touch football, surfing and boxing and was a New Zealand karate champion for three years running. He says he owes much of his athletic build to his Maori genes but genetics alone have not been enough to help him gain weight.

'I'm not sure if I have a fast metabolism or if I'm too energetic, but I'm struggling to put on weight,' he said. 'I can eat pizza six nights a week and still have the same body, without any training. I'm not on a strict diet. When I'm hungry I eat and whatever is in front of me I'll eat it.'

Nathan surfs three times a week for at least two hours at a time, does a one-hour weight-training session five times a week, plays touch football weekly and either 'runs around' or walks or plays golf once a week. He is taking a healthy approach to weight gain, combining good eating habits with regular weight training and rest. Eschewing drugs, he prefers instead to use protein and water-retention supplements.

Nathan's dedication has even stretched to paying $175 a week for pre-prepared nutritionally balanced meals. 'I usually eat six or seven meals a day, mostly chicken or meat and vegetables, and snack on fruit and raw vegetables,' he said.

Typical bodybuilders favour foods high in carbohydrates and protein, including egg-white powder, one of the highest natural protein sources. Fruit, lots of bread and vitamins and minerals (commonly Vitamin C, zinc and iron) also complement weight-training programs.

Motivation is the key, according to Nathan. 'Many guys have no idea when they come to the gym to train; they simply lift as much as they can, but you need to know what your body is experiencing and the correct foods to gain the result you're after,' he said. 'Rest is also very important, because that's when your body is growing. I try to get eight or nine hours sleep a day; I'm usually in bed by 9 p.m. and up at 5 or 6 a.m. – a carry over from my days in the New Zealand Army.

'It's a lifestyle choice if you want to achieve quality weight gain. For me, I have to rest, train and eat. If you look good then you feel well and I feel good about myself when I'm in good shape. In six or 12 months I hope to be competing in a natural body-building competition.'

During just a month of weight training, coupled with a healthy diet, Nathan gained 3 kilograms.

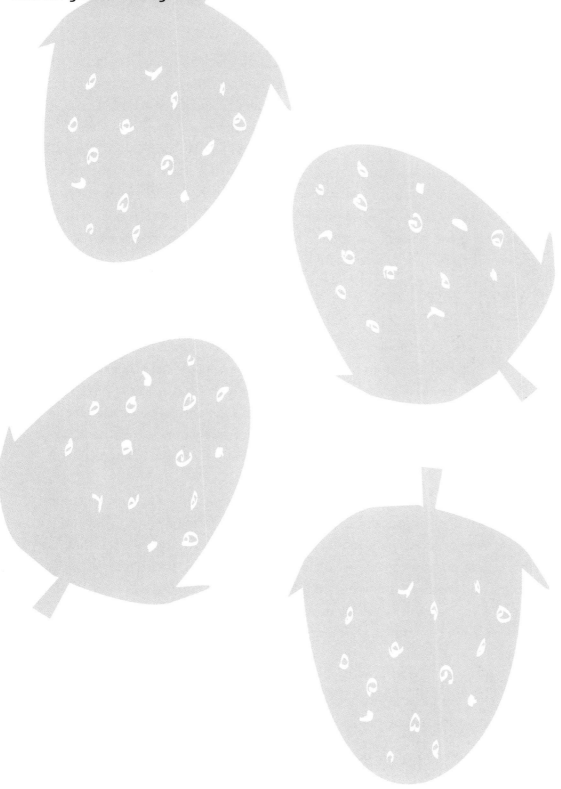

7 Nutritional supplements

Nutritional supplements are commercial products that can be used to boost the amount of nutrients (proteins, carbohydrates and fats) in your diet. They range from high-calorie drinks and weight-gain powders to complete formulas suitable for those unable to eat little else. Many supplements – and there are a wide variety – are available from supermarkets, pharmacies and health-food shops. Several can be purchased through hospitals at a discounted rate (so check with your doctor), while the larger manufacturers deliver widely. Each promises something different and some of the claims are not based on scientific evidence, so be cautious. Seek expert advice regarding the efficacy, safety and legality of the product before buying it.

Supplements are particularly useful if you can stomach little food. Some illnesses can cause digestive problems and certain medications hamper the body's absorption of particular nutrients.

Most commercial protein supplements are based on milk proteins (casein, sodium caseinate, lactoalbumin or whey powder), egg protein (albumen) or soy protein (soy isolates). Sugar (in the form of sucrose, glucose, maltodextrin, maltose, fructose or corn syrup) is added for flavour, along with fat (usually as oil) to increase calories, a general multivitamin and some kind of flavouring. Essentially, the aim of the supplement is to increase the amount of calories in your diet. Some also contain fibre, which may be useful in relieving constipation and helping control diarrhoea.

Supplements fall into two main categories. The first type usually contain one nutrient (often fibre or protein) and can be added to food or drinks. They are a convenient way of consuming more calories without dramatically altering what you eat. Then there are the complete nutritional supplements, which contain a balance of vitamins and minerals and which, if you had to, you could live on. The energy content of a supplement is usually expressed in terms of calories per millilitre.

For those keen to increase their muscle mass (athletes and sportspeople), the most useful supplement is one that provides carbohydrates (fuel) plus moderate levels of protein and other nutrients. Protein powders, all the rage in muscle-building circles, are generally too low in carbohydrates and contain excessive protein.

On the downside, supplements can be very expensive and may exacerbate other symptoms, namely diarrhoea and nausea, so it's wise to consult your dietician, doctor or pharmacist before using one. Also be sure to heed the warnings about the quantities you consume; supplements can be dangerous if taken in large doses.

Banana yoghurt shake

PUREE SOOTHING

3/4 cup (185 ml) milk or low-fat milk

3 tablespoons vanilla acidophilus yoghurt or low-fat acidophilus yoghurt

2 tablespoons skim milk powder

1 teaspoon honey

1 ripe medium banana, chopped

Combine milk, yoghurt, milk powder, honey and banana in a blender or food processor fitted with a metal blade. Blend for 1 minute or until smooth.

Pour the shake into chilled glass. Serve immediately.

Makes 1 serve.

TIP *For variety, use different flavours of fruit acidophilus yoghurts.*

REGULAR YOGHURT RECIPE
(per serve)
Kj—1460
Cal—350
Protein—17.3g
Fat—8.0g
Carbo—51.0g
Fibre—2.5g

LOW-FAT YOGHURT RECIPE
(per serve)
Kj—1300
Cal—310
Protein—20.0g
Fat—<1.0g
Carbo—56.0g
Fibre—2.5g

Prune and banana smoothie

PUREE MOVING

4 prunes, pitted

3/4 cup (185 ml) milk

1/4 cup (60 ml) fruit acidophilus yoghurt

1 ripe small banana, roughly chopped

Soak prunes in hot water for 10 minutes. Drain well.

Combine milk, yoghurt, banana and prunes in a blender or food processor fitted with a metal blade. Blend for 1 minute or until smooth.

Pour the smoothie into a chilled glass. Serve immediately.

Makes 1 serve.

TIP *Drink the water left over from soaking the prunes to help relieve the symptoms of constipation.*

(per serve)
Kj—1110
Cal—265
Protein—11.0g
Fat—7.3g
Carbo—38.7g
Fibre—2.5g

Banana and strawberry power shake

PUREE   MOVING

1/2 cup (125 ml) milk
2 tablespoons skim milk powder
1/2 lightly beaten egg (optional)
1 teaspoon wheat germ
1 small ripe banana, chopped
2 ripe strawberries, hulled and roughly chopped
1/2 teaspoon vanilla essence

Combine milk, milk powder, beaten egg, wheat germ, banana, strawberries and vanilla essence in a blender or food processor fitted with a metal blade. Blend for 1 minute or until smooth.

Pour power shake into a tall glass and serve immediately.

Makes 1 serve.

TIP *For variety, use mango, cooked peaches or apricots instead of strawberries.*

Chocolate milk shake

PUREE   MOVING

1/2 cup (125 ml) milk
2 tablespoons vanilla acidophilus yoghurt
1 tablespoon skim milk powder
1 teaspoon wheat germ
1 tablespoon chocolate drink powder plus extra for top

Combine milk, yoghurt, milk powder, wheat germ and 1 tablespoon chocolate drink powder in a blender or food processor fitted with a metal blade. Blend for about 1 minute or until smooth.

Pour milk shake into a tall glass, sprinkle top with chocolate powder and serve immediately.

Makes 1 serve.

TIP *For variety, add a scoop of chocolate or vanilla ice-cream to the milk shake.*

Fluffy scrambled egg

SOFT

(per serve)
Kj—800
Cal—191
Protein—10.2g
Fat—10.5g
Carbo—13.3g
Fibre—2.0g

1 egg
1 tablespoon milk or soy milk
pinch of salt
pinch of white pepper
1 teaspoon butter or margarine
1 slice wholemeal bread, toasted
sprig of parsley, washed and dried

In a medium bowl, beat egg, milk, salt and pepper together.

In a non-stick pan, over medium heat, melt butter or margarine. Pour in egg mixture and stir gently with a wooden spoon for about 2 minutes or until set. Serve on top of toast on a warm plate garnished with a sprig of parsley.

Makes 1 serve.

🍎 **TIPS** *To add more protein to this dish, add 1-2 more egg whites.*

If you make this dish with soy milk it will be suitable for people with lactose intolerance.

Scrambled egg with buttermilk

SOFT

(per serve)
Kj—795
Cal—190
Protein—10.4g
Fat—10.1g
Carbo—13.5g
Fibre—2.0g

1 egg, lightly beaten
1 tablespoon buttermilk
pinch of salt
pinch of pepper
1 teaspoon butter or margarine
1 slice wholemeal bread, toasted
sprig of parsley, washed and dried

In a medium bowl, beat egg, buttermilk, salt and pepper together.

In a non-stick pan, over medium heat, melt butter or margarine. Pour in egg mixture and stir gently with a wooden spoon for about 2 minutes or until set. Serve on top of toast on a warm plate garnished with a sprig of parsley.

Makes 1 serve.

(per serve)
Kj—990
Cal—237
Protein—14.6g
Fat—19.3g
Carbo—1.2g
Fibre—1.3g

Super mushroom omelette

SOFT and CHEWY

2 teaspoons olive oil
4 white mushrooms, thinly sliced
1 shallot (green onion), thinly sliced
2 eggs, separated
1 teaspoon water
pinch of salt
pinch of freshly ground pepper
1$\frac{1}{4}$ teaspoons chopped parsley

Heat 1 teaspoon oil in a non-stick frying pan over medium heat and sauté mushrooms for 2 minutes. Add shallot (green onion) and sauté for 1 minute or until cooked. Set mixture aside and keep warm.

In a medium bowl, beat egg whites until they are light and fluffy and hold their shape. Fold in lightly beaten egg yolks, water, salt, pepper and 1 teaspoon of parsley.

Preheat griller.

Heat remaining 1 teaspoon oil in a non-stick frying pan over medium heat. Pour egg mixture into pan and spread out evenly with a spatula. Cover pan with a lid and cook for 3–4 minutes or until it is set and golden brown on the bottom. Place the whole pan under the griller. When omelette has risen and turned pale brown on top, remove pan from the griller. Place mushroom mixture on omelette and fold carefully in half. Garnish with remaining $\frac{1}{4}$ teaspoon of parsley and serve.

Makes 1 serve.

STIMULATE DIGESTION
Drinking half a glass of water mixed with a teaspoon of lemon juice, 30 minutes before meals, can help stimulate digestion.

Coddled cheesy egg

SOFT

(per serve)
Kj—415
Cal—100
Protein—7.6g
Fat—7.6g
Carbo—Neg
Fibre—Neg

$^1/_2$ teaspoon butter or margarine
1 egg, at room temperature
1 teaspoon grated low-fat cheddar cheese or low-fat soy cheese
pinch of salt
pinch of white pepper

Butter the inside and metal lid of an egg coddler.

Half fill a small saucepan with water and bring to the boil.

Break the egg into the porcelain cup, sprinkle with cheese and season with salt and pepper. Screw the lid on and carefully lower into boiling water to cover to its neck. Reduce heat to simmer and cook for 7 minutes for a soft egg and 8 minutes for a firmer egg. Carefully remove lid and serve.

Makes 1 serve.

Eggs Benedict

SOFT and CHEWY

(per serve)
Kj—1270
Cal—303
Protein—23.0g
Fat—13.1g
Carbo—21.7g
Fibre—3.2g

1 wholemeal muffin, cut in half
25 g shaved ham
1 slice processed cheddar cheese
few drops of white vinegar
1 egg, at room temperature
salt and pepper to taste

Preheat the griller.

Toast muffin halves under griller until light brown. Place ham and cheese on top and toast until cheese is golden brown. Keep warm.

Meanwhile, half fill a small shallow frying pan with water, add vinegar and bring to the boil, then reduce heat to simmer. Break egg into a cup, slide it into the water, then cover the pan and cook for 2 minutes. Turn off the heat and leave pan with lid on for 2 minutes for a soft egg or 3 minutes for a firmer egg.

Remove egg using an egg slice, then drain well and place on top of a toasted cheese muffin half. Add salt and pepper to taste. Top with other muffin half. Serve immediately.

Makes 1 serve.

Prawn omelette

SOFT and CHEWY

1 egg
2 teaspoons water
pinch of white pepper
3 medium prawns, cooked, peeled, deveined and chopped
1 shallot (green onion), thinly sliced
1¹/₂ teaspoons olive oil

In a medium bowl, combine egg, water, pepper, prawns and shallot (green onion).

In a small non-stick frying pan over high heat, heat 1 teaspoon oil. Pour in egg mixture and cook, stirring the surface of the mixture with the back of a fork. Cover with a lid, reduce heat to medium–low and cook for 2 minutes or until omelette begins to brown on the bottom. Unmould and slide on to a plate. Heat remaining ¹/₂ teaspoon of oil in the same pan over high heat. Return omelette to pan, invert plate over pan browned side-up, and cook for 1 minute. Serve immediately.

Makes 1 serve.

(per serve)
Kj—525
Cal—125
Protein—10.4g
Fat—9.3g
Carbo—Neg
Fibre—Neg

Creamy egg salad

SOFT

2 eggs, at room temperature
2 teaspoons mayonnaise
¹/₂ teaspoon Dijon mustard
pinch of salt
pinch of white pepper

Carefully place eggs in a small saucepan, cover with cold water. Bring to the boil then simmer for 10 minutes. Plunge the cooked eggs into cold water, cracking the shells. When cool, peel eggs under cold running water.

In a food processor fitted with a metal blade, process eggs, mayonnaise, mustard, salt and pepper for about 2 minutes or until the mixture is smooth and creamy. Serve at room temperature within 30 minutes or cover and refrigerate for up to 2 days.

Serves 1–2.

(per serve)
Kj—885
Cal—211
Protein—13.0g
Fat—17.5g
Carbo—1.0g
Fibre—Neg

Crispy egg and yoghurt triangles

CHEWY

(per serve)
Kj—205
Cal—50
Protein—5.2g
Fat—1.9g
Carbo—2.6g
Fibre—Neg

1 egg, at room temperature
4 sheets filo pastry
40 g shaved smoked turkey
4 teaspoons plain acidophilus yoghurt or soy yoghurt
2 teaspoons snipped fresh chives
olive oil cooking spray

Preheat oven to 200°C. Line an oven tray with non-stick baking paper.

Carefully place egg in a small saucepan, cover with cold water. Bring to the boil then simmer for 10 minutes. Plunge the cooked egg into cold water, cracking the shell. When cool, peel egg under cold running water. Dice egg.

Spray a sheet of filo pastry with olive oil cooking spray and fold it in half lengthwise. Place a quarter of the egg in the lower corner. Top with a quarter of the turkey, 1 teaspoon yoghurt and sprinkle with chives. Fold filo over filling to form a triangle. Continue folding the strip of filo over the filling, keeping the triangle shape, until all pastry is wrapped around filling. Continue shaping triangles in this method and place on prepared oven tray. Spray tops with olive oil cooking spray and bake for 15–20 minutes or until puffed and golden. Serve triangles hot or warm.

Makes 4 triangles.

TIP *Cooked triangles can be kept in the refrigerator for up to 2 days. Reheat by placing into a preheated oven at 200°C for 5 minutes, or until hot and crispy.*

REGULAR MILK
RECIPE
(serve 1/3 cup)
Kj—520
Cal—124
Protein—16.7g
Fat—5.6g
Carbo—1.6g
Fibre—<1.0g

LOW-FAT MILK
RECIPE
(serve 1/3 cup)
Kj—390
Cal—93
Protein—18.0g
Fat—1.9g
Carbo—2.0g
Fibre—<1.0g

Home-made coriander cottage cheese

SOFT

1/4 cup (60 ml) fresh lemon juice
1/4 cup (60 ml) water
1/2 teaspoon vegetable oil
2 litres full-fat or low-fat milk
1/2 teaspoon salt
1/2 cup (30 g) chopped coriander

In a measuring cup, mix lemon juice and water together.

Rub the inside of a large heavy-based saucepan with oil. Add milk and salt and heat to boiling point. Stir in coriander and bring to a rolling boil, stirring constantly. Turn off heat and stir in lemon juice mixture. The milk mixture should immediately separate into curds and whey.

Carefully pour hot mixture through a colander lined with cheesecloth or muslin and set it in the sink to drain. Tie cloth with string to form a bag. Place a wooden spoon across the top of a bowl and tie ends of the bag to the spoon's handle. Let cottage cheese drain for at least 30 minutes. Use cottage cheese at room temperature or refrigerate for up 5 days in an airtight container.

Makes 1 1/2 cups cottage cheese.

TIP *Use the cottage cheese on toast, muffins or as a topping to enrich vegetable soups.*

Dill yoghurt cheese

PUREE   MOVING

(per serve)
Kj—380
Cal—91
Protein—6.8g
Fat—2.9g
Carbo—7.6g
Fibre—<1.0g

2 cups plain acidophilus yoghurt

$1/_2$ clove garlic, crushed

$1/_4$ teaspoon salt

$1/_8$ teaspoon white pepper

2 tablespoons chopped Italian (flat-leaf) parsley

1 tablespoon snipped fresh dill

$1/_2$ teaspoon paprika

Pour yoghurt into a colander lined with cheesecloth or muslin and set it over a large deep bowl. Tie cloth with string to form a bag. Place a wooden spoon across the top of the bowl and tie ends of the bag to the spoon's handle. Let drain for at least 5 hours at room temperature or overnight in the refrigerator.

Empty drained yoghurt into a bowl, add garlic, salt, pepper, parsley, dill and paprika and beat well. Cover and refrigerate for at least 2 hours before serving. Keeps up to 5 days.

Makes $1/_2$–$3/_4$ cup.

🍎 TIP The flavours of the garlic and herbs mature and strengthen the longer the cheese is kept.

Baked banana porridge

SOFT MOVING

1/2 cup (40 g) old-fashioned rolled oats

1 cup (250 ml) low-fat milk

1 egg, lightly beaten

1 ripe medium banana, mashed

1 teaspoon castor sugar

1 teaspoon vanilla essence

1/4 teaspoon cinnamon, plus pinch of cinnamon for topping

Preheat oven to 160°C. Butter 2 small ovenproof dishes.

In a medium bowl, whisk oats, milk, egg, banana, sugar, vanilla essence and 1/4 teaspoon cinnamon together. Let stand for 15 minutes. Stir again and pour mixture into prepared dishes. Sprinkle remaining cinnamon on top of porridge.

Place dishes into a larger pan. Place the pan on the middle shelf of the oven. Pour boiling water into the pan until it comes three-quarters of the way up the sides of the dishes. Bake porridge for 25–30 minutes or until golden brown and firm. Carefully remove the dishes from the larger pan and let the porridge stand for 2 minutes before serving.

Serves 2.

TIP *Refrigerate leftover porridge overnight. To reheat, cover top with plastic wrap and place in a microwave on high for 1 minute or until warmed through.*

Baked oatmeal custard with berries

PUREE and CHEWY   MOVING

(per serve)
Kj—610
Cal—145
Protein—6.6g
Fat—3.6g
Carbo—21.7g
Fibre—1.2g

$^1/_2$ cup (40 g) quick-cooking rolled oats

$^1/_2$ cup (125 ml) water

$1^1/_4$ cups (310 ml) low-fat milk

$^1/_4$ teaspoon cinnamon

2 egg yolks

$^1/_4$ cup castor sugar

$^1/_2$ teaspoon vanilla

6 ripe strawberries, hulled and roughly chopped

Preheat oven to 180°C. Butter an ovenproof casserole dish.

Combine the oats and water in a medium-size saucepan. Bring to the boil over medium-high heat, stirring constantly. Stir in $^3/_4$ cup (185 ml) of the milk and the cinnamon. Reduce heat to low and simmer, stirring frequently, for about 2 minutes or until the oats are tender. Set mixture aside to cool.

In a medium bowl, whisk egg yolks and sugar for about 5 minutes or until the mixture is light and fluffy. Stir in remaining $^1/_2$ cup (125 ml) milk, vanilla essence and porridge mixture. Pour the custard mixture into the casserole dish.

Place the casserole dish into a larger pan. Put the pan on the middle shelf of the oven. Pour boiling water into the pan until it comes three-quarters of the way up the sides of the dish. Bake custard for 30 minutes or until golden brown and firm. Carefully remove the dish from the larger pan and let the custard stand for 10 minutes before serving. Serve custard topped with strawberries.

Serves 4.

TIP *Leftover custard can be covered and refrigerated for up to 2 days.*

(per serve)
Kj—850
Cal—203
Protein—9.4g
Fat—8.4g
Carbo—22.4g
Fibre—2.3g

Banana, mango and yoghurt whip

PUREE MOVING

1 ripe small banana, roughly chopped
1 cup (250 g) fresh or canned ripe mango, cubed
2 teaspoons fresh lemon juice
1/2 cup (120 g) ricotta cheese
2 tablespoons vanilla acidophilus yoghurt

Combine banana, mango, lemon juice, ricotta cheese and yoghurt in a blender or food processor fitted with a metal blade. Blend for about 1 minute or until smooth.

Pour the whip into 2 glass bowls. Cover and refrigerate for at least 1 hour before serving.

Serves 2.

DRINK IT UP

If you can't stomach the recommended vegetable servings in their solid form, try juicing. Vegetable or fruit juices, fruit smoothies and milk shakes provide a good dose of high-calorie fluids between or with meals. Dark and thick juices are generally the highest in calories. Even soft drinks and cordial provide energy without filling you up.

Cheese soufflé

SOFT

(per serve)
Kj—1085
Cal—259
Protein—18.5g
Fat—17.1g
Carbo—8.1g
Fibre—<1.0g

¹/₂ cup (125 ml) warm milk

1 tablespoon skim milk powder

2 teaspoons butter or margarine

1 tablespoon plain wholemeal flour

2 egg yolks

¹/₄ cup (30 g) grated cheddar cheese

2 tablespoons cottage cheese

pinch of salt

pinch of pepper

pinch of nutmeg

3 egg whites

Preheat oven to 220°C. Butter 2 individual soufflé dishes – each should hold 1 cup of mixture.

In a small bowl, whisk milk and milk powder together

In a medium saucepan, melt butter. Stir in flour and cook, stirring over medium heat for 30 seconds. Remove from heat and whisk in milk and milk powder. Return to medium heat and stir constantly until mixture boils and thickens. Turn off the heat and whisk in egg yolks, one at a time. Stir in cheddar cheese, cottage cheese, salt, pepper and nutmeg.

In a large bowl, beat egg whites until they form stiff, glossy peaks. Fold egg whites carefully into cheese mixture. Pour mixture evenly into prepared soufflé dishes. Tap the bottom of each dish lightly on the kitchen bench to break any air bubbles and smooth the top of the soufflés with a spatula. Place the soufflés on a baking tray in the oven. Turn heat down to 190°C and bake for about 20 minutes or until they are puffed and golden brown. Serve immediately.

Serves 2.

10

soups & salads

Recipe	Texture	Effect on Symptom	Type	Page
Creamy carrot and ginger soup				
	PUREE	CALMING and MOVING	D, G	56
Borlotti bean and vegetable soup				
	CHEWY	MOVING	D, G, L	57
Red lentil and vegetable soup				
	CHEWY	MOVING	D, G, L	58
Corn and chicken chowder				
	CHEWY		D	59
Armenian yoghurt soup				
	PUREE	CALMING	D	60
Chicken velvet soup				
	CHEWY		D	60
Sweet potato minestrone				
	CHEWY	MOVING	D, G, L	61
Lentil and spinach soup				
	CHEWY	MOVING	D, G	62
German potato soup				
	PUREE	SOOTHING and CALMING	D, G	63
Tomato and rice soup				
	CHEWY	MOVING	D, G, L	64
Guacamole salad				
	CHEWY		G	64
Potato and beetroot salad				
	CHEWY	MOVING	D	65
Persian couscous salad				
	CRUNCHY	MOVING	D, L	66
Lemon pasta salad				
	CHEWY	MOVING	D, L	67
Russian vegetable salad				
	CHEWY	MOVING	D	68
Raw vegetable salad				
	CRUNCHY	MOVING	D	69
Jamaican pawpaw salad				
	CHEWY	MOVING		69
Cucumber and mint salad				
	CHEWY	MOVING	D, G	70
Spanish avocado salad				
	CHEWY		D, G, L	70
Avocado mousse				
	PUREE		D	71

(per serve)
Kj—950
Cal—227
Protein—8.6g
Fat—10.3g
Carbo—22.1g
Fibre—5.8g

Creamy carrot and ginger soup

SMOOTH CALMING and MOVING

1 tablespoon olive oil
$1/_2$–1 teaspoon finely grated fresh ginger
4 medium carrots, peeled and diced
1 medium potato, peeled and diced
$1/_2$ teaspoon salt
$1/_4$ teaspoon pepper
2 cups (500 ml) vegetable stock
$1/_2$ cup (125 ml) low-fat milk or low-fat soy milk
chopped parsley to garnish

In a medium saucepan, over medium heat, heat oil and sauté ginger for 30 seconds. Add carrots and potatoes and sauté for 5 minutes. Add salt, pepper and stock. Cover and bring to the boil, reduce heat and simmer uncovered for about 20 minutes or until vegetables are soft.

Transfer mixture to a blender or food processor and blend until smooth, stopping and scraping down sides of container as needed. Transfer soup to clean saucepan and add milk, reheat for 1 minute. Ladle hot soup into bowls and garnish with chopped parsley.

Serves 2–3.

TIP *Recipe can be doubled, portioned and frozen for later use.*

Borlotti bean and vegetable soup

CHEWY MOVING

(per serve)
Kj—1110
Cal—265
Protein—13.1g
Fat—6.2g
Carbo—38.1g
Fibre—6.7g

1 cup (350 g) canned borlotti beans, drained and rinsed

2 cups (500 ml) vegetable stock

2 teaspoons olive oil

1 small onion, diced

1 clove garlic, crushed (optional)

2 small carrots, peeled and diced

1 medium potato, peeled and diced

$1/2$ small parsnip, peeled and diced

$1/2$ teaspoon salt

$1/4$ teaspoon pepper

1 bay leaf

In a blender or food processor, purée beans with $1/4$ cup (60 ml) of the vegetable stock to make a creamy purée, adding a little more stock if necessary.

Heat olive oil in a medium saucepan and sauté onion for about 3 minutes or until it is golden brown. Add garlic and sauté for another 30 seconds. Add remaining vegetable stock, carrots, potato, parsnip, salt, pepper, bay leaf and bean purée. Bring to the boil, then cover and simmer for 30–40 minutes or until vegetables are tender, stirring occasionally to prevent them sticking to the bottom of the pan. Remove the bay leaf.

The soup can be served chunky or puréed in a blender or food processor to a smooth texture.

Serves 2–3.

TIP *Recipe can be doubled, portioned and frozen for later use.*

Red lentil and vegetable soup

CHEWY MOVING

2 teaspoons olive oil
1 medium onion, finely diced
$^1/_2$ teaspoon paprika
$^1/_2$ teaspoon ground cumin
$^1/_2$ teaspoon ground coriander
$^1/_2$ teaspoon turmeric
$^1/_2$ teaspoon cayenne pepper (optional)
$^1/_3$ cup (75 g) red lentils, rinsed
1 medium potato, peeled and grated
1 cup (120 g) grated butternut pumpkin
3–3$^1/_2$ cups (750–875 ml) vegetable stock
$^1/_2$ teaspoon salt

Heat oil in a medium heavy-based saucepan over medium heat and sauté onions for about 3 minutes or until translucent. Add paprika, cumin, coriander, turmeric and cayenne pepper (if using) and sauté for 30 seconds. Add lentils, potato, pumpkin, 3 cups (750 ml) of stock and salt and bring to the boil, stirring frequently. Reduce heat to simmer and cook for about 30–40 minutes or until lentils are soft, stirring occasionally. Add extra $^1/_2$ cup (125 ml) of stock if mixture becomes too thick. Ladle hot soup into bowls and serve.

Serves 3–4.

ADD ZING AND ZEST
Try using herbs and spices (chilli and cayenne pepper give any meal a lift) in your cooking for flavour and interest; some even help aid digestion. Also consider the colour and texture of ingredients to add zing and zest.

Corn and chicken chowder

CHEWY

(per serve)
Kj—995
Cal—238
Protein—17.9g
Fat—6.7g
Carbo—24.6g
Fibre—3.3g

1¹/₂ cups (375 ml) chicken stock
1 medium potato, peeled and diced
¹/₂ small onion, diced
¹/₂ stalk celery, diced (optional)
¹/₂ cup (60 g) corn kernels
¹/₂ cup (125 ml) milk or soy milk
1 tablespoon plain wholemeal flour
¹/₂ cup (125 g) cooked diced chicken
1 tablespoon chopped parsley

In a medium saucepan, bring stock, potato, onion, celery and corn to a boil over high heat. Reduce heat and simmer for 30 minutes or until vegetables are soft. Cool mixture.

In a medium bowl, blend milk and flour together to a thin, smooth paste.

Transfer potato mixture to a blender or food processor fitted with the metal blade and blend until smooth, stopping and scraping down sides of container as needed. Transfer soup to clean saucepan and add milk mixture and chicken. Reheat soup, stirring constantly, for about 3–4 minutes or until thickened. Ladle hot soup into bowls and garnish with chopped parsley.

Serves 2.

🍎 **TIP** *If you make this dish with soy milk it will be suitable for people with lactose intolerance.*

(per serve)
Kj—495
Cal—118
Protein—10.5g
Fat—3.7g
Carbo—9.7g
Fibre—Neg

Armenian yoghurt soup

PUREE   CALMING

2 cups (500 ml) chicken stock
1/4 cup fine egg noodles
1 egg, lightly beaten
1/2 cup (125 ml) plain low-fat acidophilus yoghurt
pinch of paprika

In a medium saucepan, bring stock and noodles to a boil, reduce heat to simmer and cook for about 5 minutes or until noodles are tender.

In a bowl, beat egg and yoghurt together. Slowly beat 1/2 cup (125 ml) of boiling soup into yoghurt mixture, then add this yoghurt mixture to the soup. Heat through but do not boil. Sprinkle top with paprika and serve immediately.

Serves 2.

(per serve)
Kj—1445
Cal—345
Protein—22.3g
Fat—19.2g
Carbo—21.3g
Fibre—<1.0g

Chicken velvet soup

CHEWY

1 tablespoon butter or margarine
1 1/2 tablespoons plain flour
1/2 cup (125 ml) low-fat milk
1/2 cup (125 ml) chicken stock
60 g chicken breast fillet, finely chopped
pinch of black pepper
salt to taste
1 teaspoon chopped parsley

In a medium saucepan, melt butter. Stir in flour and cook, stirring, over medium heat for 30 seconds. Remove from heat and whisk in milk and chicken stock. Return to medium heat and stir constantly until mixture boils and thickens. Reduce heat and stir in chopped chicken, pepper and salt. Return soup to the boil, then reduce to simmer and cook for about 5 minutes or until chicken is cooked. Adjust seasoning, garnish with parsley and serve.

Serves 1–2.

Sweet potato minestrone

CHEWY MOVING

(per serve)
Kj—490
Cal—117
Protein—4.4g
Fat—2.9g
Carbo—16.0g
Fibre—4.4g

2 teaspoons olive oil

1 small onion, diced

1 stalk celery, diced

1/2 teaspoon dried oregano

1/2 teaspoon dried basil

1 × 400 g can chopped tomatoes in tomato juice

2 cups (500 ml) vegetable stock

250 g sweet potato, peeled and diced

2 carrots, peeled and diced

1 clove garlic, crushed (optional)

1/4 teaspoon salt

1/4 teaspoon pepper

1/2 cup (75 g) sliced green beans

Heat oil in a medium heavy-based saucepan over medium heat and sauté
onion for about 3 minutes or until translucent. Add celery, oregano and basil
and sauté for 30 seconds. Add tomatoes and juice, vegetable stock, sweet
potato, carrots, garlic, salt and pepper and bring to the boil, stirring
occasionally. Reduce heat to simmer and cook for about 30–40 minutes or
until vegetables are soft. Add beans and cook for 5 minutes. Adjust
seasoning and serve.

Serves 3–4.

Lentil and spinach soup

CHEWY   MOVING

(per serve)
Kj—730
Cal—174
Protein—12.5g
Fat—5.0g
Carbo—17.2g
Fibre—6.1g

2 teaspoons olive oil

1 medium onion, finely diced

$^1/_4$ teaspoon turmeric

$^1/_4$ teaspoon ground cumin

$^1/_4$ teaspoon ground coriander

$^1/_2$ cup (100 g) brown lentils, rinsed

1 medium vine-ripened tomato, diced

3–3$^1/_2$ cups (750–875 ml) vegetable stock

1 cup English spinach, stems removed, rinsed, dried and roughly chopped

$^1/_4$ teaspoon salt

$^1/_4$ teaspoon pepper

2 tablespoons plain acidophilus yoghurt, for serving

Heat oil in a medium heavy-based saucepan over medium heat and sauté onions for about 3 minutes or until translucent. Add turmeric, cumin and coriander and sauté for 10 seconds. Add lentils, diced tomato and 3 cups (750 ml) of stock and bring to the boil, stirring frequently. Reduce heat to simmer and cook for about 30–40 minutes or until lentils are soft, stirring occasionally. Add extra stock if mixture becomes too thick. Stir in spinach, salt and pepper and simmer, covered with a tight-fitting lid, for about 5 minutes or until spinach has wilted and cooked. Ladle the hot soup into bowls and top each bowl with 1 tablespoon yoghurt.

Serves 2–3.

TIPS *This soup can be covered with plastic wrap, refrigerated and kept for up to 3 days.*

If you do not top the soup with yoghurt, the dish is suitable for those who are lactose intolerant.

German potato soup

PUREE   SOOTHING and CALMING

(per serve)
Kj—1300
Cal—310
Protein—7.8g
Fat—20.0g
Carbo—23.3g
Fibre—3.7g

1 tablespoon olive oil

2 medium potatoes, peeled and roughly diced

1 carrot, peeled and finely diced

1 stick celery, diced (optional)

1¹/₂ cups (375 ml) hot vegetable stock

¹/₂ teaspoon salt

1 bay leaf

1 tablespoon butter or margarine

¹/₂ cup (125 ml) milk

1 tablespoon chopped parsley

Heat oil in a medium heavy-based saucepan over medium heat and sauté potatoes, carrot and celery for about 5 minutes. Add hot vegetable stock, salt and bay leaf, bring to the boil, then cover and reduce heat to simmer for about 20–30 minutes or until vegetables are tender. Remove bay leaf and purée vegetables and cooking liquid with a ricer or potato masher until they are creamy. Add butter and stir well.

In a medium saucepan, over medium heat, warm puréed vegetables with milk and simmer for 5 minutes. Adjust seasoning.

Ladle hot soup into bowls and garnish with parsley.

Serves 2–3.

🍎 TIP   *This soup keeps for up to 3 days in the refrigerator.*

Tomato and rice soup

CHEWY MOVING

(per serve)
Kj—550
Cal—131
Protein—3.2g
Fat—6.8g
Carbo—12.1g
Fibre—2.6g

1 tablespoon olive oil
1 small onion, finely diced
3 tablespoons raw brown rice
2 cups (500 ml) beef stock
1 × 400 g can chopped tomatoes in tomato juice
salt and pepper to taste
2 tablespoons chopped flat-leaf (Italian) parsley

Heat oil in a medium, heavy-based saucepan over medium heat and sauté onion for about 3 minutes or until translucent. Add rice and sauté for 1 minute. Add beef stock, tomatoes and juice, salt and pepper and bring to the boil, stirring occasionally. Reduce heat to simmer and cook for about 40–50 minutes or until rice is cooked. Adjust seasoning and ladle soup into bowls. Garnish with parsley and serve hot.

Serves 2–3.

Guacamole salad

CHEWY

(per serve)
Kj—1720
Cal—411
Protein—5.7g
Fat—40.4g
Carbo—5.0g
Fibre—3.2g

1/2 ripe avocado, peeled
2 teaspoons fresh lemon juice
1/4 cup (60 ml) light sour cream
few drops Tabasco (optional)
1 cup mixed lettuce leaves, washed and torn apart
1/2 small vine-ripened tomato, diced
freshly ground black pepper

In a small bowl, mash avocado with a fork or potato masher. Add lemon juice, sour cream and Tabasco and mix well.

On a plate, arrange lettuce, top with guacamole and garnish with tomato and pepper and serve.

Makes 1 serve.

Potato and beetroot salad

CHEWY MOVING

(per serve)
Kj—885
Cal—211
Protein—4.6g
Fat—2.8g
Carbo—24.1g
Fibre—4.7g

Salad

2 medium waxy potatoes (e.g. Desiree), boiled, peeled and cubed

2 small beetroot, boiled, peeled and cubed

1 hard-boiled egg, diced

1 shallot (green onion), finely chopped

Dressing

2 tablespoons plain low-fat acidophilus yoghurt

2 tablespoons low-fat mayonnaise

1 teaspoon finely chopped parsley

1 teaspoon Dijon mustard

1/4 teaspoon salt

1/4 teaspoon pepper

To prepare dressing: in a small bowl, mix yoghurt, mayonnaise, parsley, mustard, salt and pepper together.

In a medium bowl, mix potatoes, beetroot, egg and shallot (green onion) together. Mix dressing into salad. Cover and refrigerate for at least 1 hour before serving.

Serves 2–4.

BE FLEXIBLE

Some symptoms – such as nausea and diarrhoea – may not persist indefinitely. Avoid certain foods that exacerbate your symptoms while you experience them, then resume normal healthy eating patterns once you're on the mend.

(per serve)
Kj—1085
Cal—260
Protein—3.7g
Fat—14.3g
Carbo—27.8g
Fibre—3.5g

Persian couscous salad

CRUNCHY MOVING

Salad

³/₄ cup (185 ml) boiling water

¹/₂ cup (100 g) couscous

pinch of salt

¹/₄ cup (30 g) currants

4 dried apricots, diced

¹/₄ cup (30 g) sultanas

3 prunes, pitted and diced

¹/₂ small red-skinned apple, cored and diced

¹/₄ cup (30 g) chopped toasted almonds

Dressing

2 tablespoons olive oil

2 tablespoons fresh orange juice

2 teaspoons fresh lemon juice

1 teaspoon sugar (optional)

2 tablespoons chopped mint

¹/₄ teaspoon cinnamon

¹/₂ teaspoon salt

In a large bowl, mix water, couscous and salt together. Let the mixture stand, covered, for about 5 minutes or until liquid is absorbed. Fluff couscous mixture with a fork. Add currants, apricots, sultanas, prunes, apple and almonds and mix well.

To make dressing, in a small jar with a screw-top lid, combine oil, orange juice, lemon juice, sugar, mint, cinnamon, and salt and shake until blended.

Pour dressing over salad and toss well. Cover and refrigerate for up to 3 hours for flavours to develop before serving, or overnight.

Serves 3–4.

Lemon pasta salad

CHEWY MOVING

(per serve)
Kj—845
Cal—202
Protein—4.5g
Fat—9.9g
Carbo—22.2g
Fibre—2.8g

Salad

3/4 cup (100 g) dry, elbow-shaped macaroni

1 cup (180 g) broccoli florets

1 medium carrot, peeled and diced

1 medium zucchini, diced

6 black olives, pitted and chopped

1 tablespoon chopped parsley

1 teaspoon snipped chives

Dressing

2 tablespoons olive oil

2 teaspoons fresh lemon juice

1 teaspoon Dijon mustard

1/4–1/2 teaspoon salt

In a medium saucepan of salted boiling water, cook macaroni for about 8–10 minutes or until tender. Drain well and cool.

Steam broccoli for about 5 minutes or until crisp but tender. Steam carrot for about 5 minutes or until crisp but tender. Steam zucchini for about 3 minutes or until crisp but tender.

In a large bowl, mix macaroni, broccoli, carrot, zucchini, olives, parsley and chives together.

To make dressing: in a small jar with a screw-top lid, combine oil, lemon juice, mustard and salt and shake until blended.

Pour dressing over salad and toss well. Cover and refrigerate for up to 3 hours for flavours to develop before serving, or overnight.

Serves 3–4.

Russian vegetable salad

CHEWY MOVING

(per serve)
Kj—850
Cal—203
Protein—10.7g
Fat—5.8g
Carbo—23.5g
Fibre—5.8g

Salad

1 medium waxy potato (e.g. Desiree), peeled and diced

1/2 cup (75 g) sliced green beans

1/2 cup (60 g) frozen peas, defrosted

1/4 cup (30 g) corn kernels

1 small carrot, peeled and diced

1 hard-boiled egg, diced

1 shallot (green onion), finely chopped

1 teaspoon snipped fresh dill

Dressing

1/4 cup (60 ml) plain low-fat acidophilus yoghurt

2 tablespoons low-fat mayonnaise

1 teaspoon finely chopped parsley

1 teaspoon Dijon mustard

1/4 teaspoon salt

1/4 teaspoon pepper

Cook each vegetable separately in salted, boiling water until just tender, about 3–5 minutes. Drain and let cool.

In a large bowl, mix cooked vegetables, egg and shallot (green onion). Drizzle with a bit of oil and vinegar, and mix well.

To prepare dressing: in a small bowl, mix yoghurt, mayonnaise, parsley, mustard, salt and pepper together.

Mix dressing into salad. Cover and refrigerate for at least 1 hour before serving, for flavours to develop.

Serves 2–4.

Raw vegetable salad

CRUNCHY MOVING

(per serve)
Kj—415
Cal—100
Protein—4.7g
Fat—<1.0g
Carbo—16.0g
Fibre—5.0g

Salad

1 cup (100 g) finely shredded green cabbage

1 small beetroot, washed and scrubbed, grated with a box grater

1 medium carrot, peeled and grated with a box grater

1/2 red-skinned apple, cored and grated with a box grater

Dressing

2 tablespoons buttermilk

1/4 cup (60 ml) plain acidophilus yoghurt

3 tablespoons fresh orange juice

1/2 clove garlic, crushed (optional)

1 teaspoon Dijon mustard

1/2 teaspoon salt

pinch of pepper

In a large bowl, mix cabbage, beetroot, carrot and apple together.

To prepare dressing: in a blender or food processor, combine buttermilk, yoghurt, orange juice, garlic (if using), mustard, salt and pepper. Blend for 30 seconds. Pour dressing over vegetables and mix well. Cover and refrigerate for up to 4 hours, for flavours to develop, before serving.

Serves 2–3.

Jamaican pawpaw salad

CHEWY MOVING

(per serve)
Kj—695
Cal—167
Protein—2.1g
Fat—13.8g
Carbo—7.0g
Fibre—3.4g

1/2 cup mixed lettuce, washed and dried

1 cup ripe pawpaw (250g), peeled, pitted and cut into 2.5 cm cubes

1/2 vine-ripened tomato, diced

1/2 ripe avocado, diced

1 tablespoon chopped coriander

pinch of salt

1 tablespoon fresh lime or orange juice

Arrange lettuce leaves on 2 plates.

In a medium bowl, mix pawpaw, tomato, avocado, coriander and salt together. Drizzle with lime juice and mix well. Divide pawpaw mixture between plates. Serve immediately.

Serves 2.

Cucumber and mint salad

CHEWY MOVING

(per serve)
Kj—90
Cal—22
Protein—1.7g
Fat—<1.0g
Carbo—2.7g
Fibre—<1.0g

2 Lebanese cucumbers, peeled, seeded and grated with a box grater
1/4 cup (60 ml) plain acidophilus yoghurt
2 tablespoons chopped mint
pinch of salt
pinch of pepper

Squeeze grated cucumber with hands to remove excess liquid. Place in a medium bowl.

In a small bowl, mix yoghurt, mint, salt and pepper together. Add yoghurt mixture to cucumber and mix well. Cover and refrigerate to chill before serving, for up to 4 hours.

Serves 2–3.

Spanish avocado salad

CHEWY

(per serve)
Kj—2210
Cal—528
Protein—6.8g
Fat—45.6g
Carbo—19.7g
Fibre—5.6g

1/2 ripe avocado, peeled and diced
1 tablespoon fresh lime or lemon juice
1 cup mixed lettuce leaves, washed and torn apart
1/2 vine-ripened tomato, diced
1 tablespoon chopped red (Spanish) onion
1 small potato, peeled, cooked and diced
salt and pepper to taste
1 tablespoon olive oil
1 teaspoon balsamic vinegar

Combine avocado with lime or lemon juice.

In a bowl, toss lettuce, avocado, tomato, onion and potato together. Season with salt and pepper. Just before serving, drizzle oil and vinegar over the salad and toss well.

Makes 1 serve.

Avocado mousse

PUREE

³/₄ teaspoon gelatine

¹/₄ cup (60 ml) hot chicken stock

¹/₂ large ripe avocado, peeled and mashed

¹/₂ teaspoon snipped chives (optional)

2 teaspoons fresh lemon juice

few drops Worcestershire sauce

few drops Tabasco

1 egg white

2 tablespoons plain acidophilus yoghurt

2 tablespoons mayonnaise

paprika for serving

(per serve)
Kj—930
Cal—222
Protein—5.5g
Fat—18.5g
Carbo—5.4g
Fibre—1.0g

Oil 2 x ¹/₂ cup (125 ml) moulds with vegetable oil.

In a small heatproof bowl, soften gelatine in 2 tablespoons chicken stock. Either place the bowl in the microwave on high power for 15 seconds and stir well to dissolve gelatine, or place the bowl in a saucepan of boiling water, stirring the mixture until gelatine dissolves.

In a medium bowl, mix gelatine mixture, remaining chicken stock, avocado, chives, lemon juice, Worcestershire sauce, Tabasco, salt and pepper together. Chill the mixture in the refrigerator for about 30 minutes or until it is the consistency of unbeaten egg whites.

In a large bowl, beat egg white until it forms stiff, glossy peaks. Fold egg white into avocado mixture. Fold yoghurt and mayonnaise into avocado mixture. Pour mixture into prepared moulds. Dust tops with paprika and refrigerate until mousse is set, about 4 hours.

Serves 2.

11

grains, pasta & rice

Recipe	Texture	Effect on Symptom	Type	Page
Quinoa with fruit porridge	SOFT	MOVING	D, L	74
Farina porridge	SOFT	MOVING	D	74
Barley with mushrooms	CHEWY	MOVING	D, G, L	75
Barley and tomato stew	CHEWY	MOVING	D, G, L	76
Buckwheat noodles with tomato sauce	FIRM	MOVING	D, G	77
Rice noodles with tofu and vegetables	CHEWY and CRUNCHY	MOVING	D, L	78
Baked macaroni with cheese	SOFT and CHEWY		D	79
Spaghetti with quick Bolognese sauce	CHEWY		D	80
Capellini with creamy bacon sauce	CHEWY		D	81
Vermicelli with scallops Portuguese	CHEWY		D	82
Spanish rice with avocado	SOFT		D, G, L	83
Green rice with tomatoes	SOFT	MOVING	D, G, L	84
Cheesy tuna rice	SOFT		D, G	85
Asparagus and lentil risotto	SOFT and CHEWY	MOVING	D, G	86
Breakfast kasha with milk	SOFT	MOVING	D, G	87

(per serve)
Kj—860
Cal—205
Protein—3.5g
Fat—1.5g
Carbo—43.4g
Fibre—2.6g

Quinoa with fruit porridge

SOFT MOVING

$^1/_4$ cup (40 g) quinoa

$^3/_4$ cup (185 ml) water

2 teaspoons honey

$^1/_4$ cup (40 g) old-fashioned rolled oats

$^3/_4$ cup (185 ml) unsweetened pineapple juice

2 teaspoons sultanas

2 dried apricots, diced

2 prunes, pitted and diced

Place quinoa in a colander and rinse under cold water and drain well.

In a medium saucepan, bring water and honey to the boil. Stir in quinoa and bring to the boil over medium-high heat, stirring constantly. Reduce heat to low and simmer, stirring occasionally for 10 minutes. Stir in oats, pineapple juice, sultanas, apricots and prunes and simmer for another 15 minutes or until quinoa is soft, stirring occasionally. Pour the porridge into warm bowls.

Serves 1–2.

 TIP *Quinoa (pronounced keen-wa) is a grain traditionally grown in the Andes by South American Indians and is high in vegetable protein. It can be obtained at health-food shops and should be stored in an airtight container in a cool place.*

(per serve)
Kj—780
Cal—186
Protein—13.3g
Fat—3.3g
Carbo—24.9g
Fibre—<1.0g

Farina porridge

SOFT MOVING

1 cup (250 ml) low-fat or whole milk

1 tablespoon Farina

pinch of salt

1 teaspoon butter

In a small saucepan, bring milk to a boil. Reduce heat to low and stir in Farina and salt. Stir the mixture constantly for about 2 minutes or until it is the consistency of thick sour cream. Pour into bowl and top with butter. Serve immediately.

Makes 1 serve.

Barley with mushrooms

CHEWY MOVING

(per serve)
Kj—710
Cal—170
Protein—4.9g
Fat—5.1g
Carbo—22.7g
Fibre—10.4g

2 teaspoons olive oil

1 clove garlic, crushed (optional)

4 button mushrooms, sliced

1 teaspoon lemon juice

1 vine-ripened tomato, diced

2 teaspoons tomato paste

2 tablespoons water

salt and pepper to taste

1 cup hot cooked pearl barley

2 teaspoons chopped parsley

In a medium non-stick frying pan, over medium heat, heat oil and sauté garlic for 15 seconds. Add mushrooms and sauté for 2–3 minutes. Stir in lemon juice and cook for 30 seconds. Add tomato, tomato paste, water, salt and pepper and cook, stirring occasionally, for 3–4 minutes. Add barley and cook for a further 3 minutes. Put on warm plates, garnish with parsley and serve.

Serves 1–2.

BE PREPARED

The commitment to gaining weight will require weekly meal planning and dedicated grocery shopping. But don't make it too onerous. Consider preparing ingredients in advance. Pre-wash fruit and vegetables, and slice or dice them for storage in airtight containers in the fridge – ready for cooking.

Spanish rice with avocado

SOFT

(per serve)
Kj—1400
Cal—334
Protein—5.1g
Fat—24.7g
Carbo—22.4g
Fibre—2.0g

1 teaspoon butter

1 teaspoon olive oil

$1/2$ small onion, finely diced

1 clove garlic, crushed (optional)

$1/8$ teaspoon dried oregano

$1/8$ teaspoon ground cumin

$1/8$ teaspoon turmeric

$1/4$ cup (50 g) basmati or long-grain rice

$1/2$ cup (125 ml) chicken stock

1 small ripe avocado, peeled and diced

In a heavy-based saucepan, over medium heat, melt butter with oil and sauté onion for about 3 minutes or golden. Add garlic and sauté for 30 seconds. Add oregano, cumin, turmeric and sauté for 10 seconds. Add rice and cook for 1 minute, stirring constantly. Stir in chicken stock and bring to the boil, stirring occasionally. Reduce heat, cover with a tight-fitting lid and simmer for about 15 minutes until stock is absorbed and rice is tender.

Turn off heat, fluff up rice with a fork and gently fold in avocado. Let stand for 5 minutes before serving.

Serves 2.

OLD FAVOURITES
Tempt your tastebuds with your favourite foods when you're feeling well. Avoid the favourites when you are unwell; you don't want to start associating those foods with illness.

(per serve)
Kj—1060
Cal—253
Protein—5.8g
Fat—9.9g
Carbo—33.8g
Fibre—2.8g

Green rice with tomatoes

SOFT MOVING

1 tablespoon olive oil

1 small onion, finely diced

1 clove garlic, crushed

$^1/_2$ cup (100 g) long-grain rice

2 teaspoons finely chopped parsley

1 cup washed and finely chopped English spinach

1 cup (250 ml) vegetable stock or water

1 tablespoon tomato paste

1 vine-ripened tomato, finely diced

pinch of salt

pinch of pepper

In a medium-sized saucepan, heat oil over medium heat and sauté onion for about 3 minutes or until golden brown. Stir in garlic and sauté for 30 seconds. Stir in rice and cook, stirring constantly, for 1 minute. Add parsley and spinach and cook for 15 seconds. Add stock, tomato paste, diced tomato, salt and pepper and bring to the boil, stirring occasionally. Reduce heat, cover with a tight-fitting lid and simmer for about 20–25 minutes or until stock is absorbed and rice is tender. Turn off heat and leave with the lid on for 5 minutes before serving.

Serves 2–3.

TIP *Leftover rice can be stored in the refrigerator in an airtight container for up to 2 days and reheated in a microwave oven on high for 1 minute or until hot.*

Cheesy tuna rice

SOFT

(per serve)
Kj—1235
Cal—295
Protein—22.1g
Fat—9.8g
Carbo—29.1g
Fibre—<1.0g

$^1/_2$ cup (125 ml) water

$^1/_2$ cup (125 ml) milk

$^1/_8$ teaspoon salt

$^1/_8$ teaspoon dill seeds

$^1/_2$ cup (100 g) long-grain rice

$^1/_2$ cup (100 g) canned tuna in oil, drained and flaked

$^1/_2$ cup (60 g) grated low-fat cheddar cheese

1 tablespoon chopped parsley

Combine the water, milk, salt and dill seeds in a medium-sized saucepan. Bring to the boil over medium-high heat. Add rice and tuna and stir well. Bring to the boil, reduce heat, cover with a tight-fitting lid and simmer for about 15–20 minutes or until stock is absorbed and rice is tender. Turn off heat, fold in cheese and parsley and leave with the lid on for 5 minutes before serving.

Serves 2–3.

(per serve)
Kj—775
Cal—185
Protein—5.6g
Fat—3.8g
Carbo—31.3g
Fibre—2.2g

Asparagus and lentil risotto

SOFT and CHEWY   MOVING

6 spears asparagus, cut into 2.5 cm pieces
2 teaspoons olive oil
1 small onion, finely diced
1/2 cup (75 g) cooked brown lentils
2 1/2 cups (625 ml) boiling chicken stock or water
1/2 cup (115 g) arborio rice
1 teaspoon grated parmesan cheese

Steam asparagus for 2 minutes. Set aside.

In a medium-sized saucepan, heat oil over medium heat and sauté onion for about 3 minutes or until golden brown. Stir in lentils and sauté for 30 seconds. Add 1/2 cup (125 ml) stock and boil for 5 minutes. Stir in rice. Gradually add rest of boiling stock, 1/2 cup at a time, stirring until liquid has been absorbed before adding the next 1/2 cup. Fold through asparagus, heat for 3–4 minutes more. Serve with cheese.

Serves 2–3.

TIP *It should take about 35–40 minutes for the rice to cook and soften.*

Breakfast kasha with milk

SOFT MOVING

½ cup (100 g) kasha (roasted buckwheat)
1 egg, beaten
2 teaspoons vegetable oil
pinch of salt
1–1¼ cups (250–310 ml) milk plus extra milk for serving
1 teaspoon butter

Mix kasha with beaten egg. In a heavy, non-stick saucepan, over medium heat, heat oil, add kasha and stir with a wooden spoon until egg is cooked. Stir in salt and 1 cup (250 ml) milk, bring the mixture to the boil, lower heat to simmer, cover saucepan with a tight-fitting lid and cook for about 20–25 minutes or until kasha is soft, stirring occasionally. Add remaining ¼ cup (60 ml) milk if needed. Pour into bowls and top with butter. Serve with extra milk.

Serves 1–2.

MILK IT
A simple way of adding calories, protein and calcium to your meals is to substitute milk for water. Try it in hot cereal, soups and sauces, or sprinkle powdered milk into casseroles and meatloaf.

(per serve)
Kj—1410
Cal—337
Protein—12.7g
Fat—14.8g
Carbo—38.5g
Fibre—1.3g

12

meat, poultry & seafood

Recipe	Texture	Effect on Symptom	Type	Page
Beef goulash				
	CHEWY		D, L	90
Braised beef with red wine				
	CHEWY		D, L	91
Braised lamb shanks				
	CHEWY		L	92
Lamb chops with prunes				
	CHEWY	MOVING	D, G, L	93
Shepherd's pie				
	SOFT		D	94
Sautéed liver with onions				
	FIRM and CHEWY		L	95
Chicken and mushroom pie				
	CHEWY		D	96
Chicken with broccoli				
	CHEWY	MOVING	D, L	98
Chicken with dill sauce and bow-tie noodles				
	CHEWY		D, L	99
Cantonese chicken with cellophane noodles				
	CHEWY		D, L	100
Liver dumplings with chicken soup				
	SOFT	SOOTHING	D	101
Creamy prawn bisque				
	PUREE		G	102
Italian fried fish with lemon sauce				
	CHEWY			103
Seafood in cheese sauce with pasta				
	CHEWY		D	104
Barbecued salmon on English spinach				
	CHEWY	MOVING	D, L	105

On a floured board, roll out pastry to size that covers dishes with excess of 2 cm. Moisten the rim of the dishes with water and firmly press lid of pastry into place. Cut small vents in the middle of the pastry. Brush tops with beaten egg yolk. Bake for 10 minutes then reduce heat to 180°C and bake for a further 20 minutes.

Serves 2.

 TIP *Use chicken stock for other recipes. It can be frozen in ice-cube trays or refrigerated for up to 3 days.*

TWICE THE TASTE

Increase the calorie content of sandwiches by doubling up on your fillings. Mixing sweet and savoury ingredients can create tasty combinations like cheese and marmalade, peanut butter and raisins, creamed cheese and pineapple, or avocado and bacon.

(per serve)
Kj—2340
Cal—559
Protein—31.2g
Fat—28.0g
Carbo—43.8g
Fibre—4.1g

Chicken with broccoli

CHEWY MOVING

4 teaspoons vegetable oil

250 g boneless chicken thighs, all fat and gristle removed, cut into 2.5 cm pieces

1/2 small onion, sliced

1 clove garlic, crushed

1 small carrot, peeled and thinly sliced

1 cup (180 g) broccoli florets

1 teaspoon cornflour

1/2 cup (125 ml) chicken stock

2 teaspoons light soy sauce

1 teaspoon oyster sauce

1/4 cup unsalted roasted cashew nuts

1 1/2 cups hot cooked rice

Heat 2 teaspoons of oil in a wok or non-stick frying pan over high heat, then stir-fry chicken for 3–4 minutes or until light brown. Remove chicken and set aside.

Heat the remaining 2 teaspoons oil and stir-fry onion for 1 minute. Add garlic and stir-fry for 30 seconds. Add carrot and broccoli and stir-fry for about 5 minutes or until carrots are tender.

In a small bowl, mix cornflour, chicken stock, soy sauce and oyster sauce together. Return chicken to wok, then add cornflour mixture and stir until liquid boils and thickens slightly. Serve immediately on hot rice and garnish with cashew nuts.

Serves 2.

Chicken with dill sauce and bow-tie noodles

CHEWY

(per serve)
Kj—2880
Cal—688
Protein—39.4g
Fat—26.0g
Carbo—71.5g
Fibre—3.7g

200 g dry bow-tie noodles

2 teaspoons vegetable oil

250 g chicken breast fillet, excess fat removed, cut into 2.5 cm pieces

1 clove garlic, crushed (optional)

2 teaspoons cornflour

$^1/_4$ cup (60 ml) cream

$^1/_2$ cup (125 ml) chicken stock

$2^1/_2$ teaspoons chopped fresh dill

1 teaspoon fresh lemon juice

salt to taste

pepper to taste

In a pot of salted boiling water, cook bow-ties for about 10–12 minutes or until tender. Drain well, set aside and keep warm.

Heat oil in a wok or non-stick frying pan over high heat and stir-fry chicken for 3–4 minutes or until light brown. Add garlic and stir-fry for 30 seconds.

In a small bowl, mix cornflour, cream, chicken stock and 2 teaspoons of dill together. Add cornflour mixture to wok and stir until liquid boils and thickens slightly. Turn off heat and stir in lemon juice, salt and pepper. Serve immediately on hot bow-tie noodles and garnish with extra dill.

Serves 2.

Cantonese chicken with cellophane noodles

CHEWY

150 g cellophane rice noodles
2 teaspoons soy sauce
1 tablespoon tomato paste
1/3 cup (80 ml) chicken stock
2 teaspoons vegetable oil
200 g boneless chicken thighs, all fat and gristle removed, cut into 2.5 cm pieces
1 clove garlic, crushed
1/2 teaspoon grated fresh ginger
2 shallots (green onion), finely sliced

Cover the noodles with hot water for about 10 minutes or until they are very soft. Drain well in a colander. Set aside.

In a small bowl, mix soy sauce, tomato paste and chicken stock together.

Heat 1 teaspoon of oil in a wok or non-stick frying pan over high heat and stir-fry chicken for 2–3 minutes or until light brown. Remove chicken and set aside.

Heat remaining teaspoon of oil in a wok and stir-fry garlic and ginger for 30 seconds. Add chicken, shallots (green onion) and the soy sauce mixture and bring to the boil. Reduce heat to simmer and cook for about 3–4 minutes or until chicken is tender and cooked through. Serve immediately on hot cellophane noodles.

Serves 2.

EAT UP!

Liver dumplings with chicken soup

SOFT SOOTHING

(per serve)
Kj—840
Cal—201
Protein—16.6g
Fat—4.8g
Carbo—22.1g
Fibre—2.0g

100 g chicken livers, excess fat and gristle removed
1 teaspoon finely grated onion
1 egg yolk
pinch of salt
pinch of pepper
pinch of nutmeg
3 teaspoons chopped parsley
1 slice wholemeal bread, crusts removed
$^1/_4$ cup (60 ml) milk
$^1/_4$ cup (30 g) plain flour
3 cups (750 ml) chicken stock

Mince or finely chop liver with onion. Add egg yolk, salt, pepper, nutmeg and 2 teaspoons of parsley.

Soak bread in milk for 10 minutes. Squeeze out excess milk from bread and add bread to liver mixture, then mix flour into liver mixture, stirring until a soft dough.

In a medium saucepan, bring stock to the boil. Dip a teaspoon into the stock, then fill it with liver dough and drop into stock. Re-dip the spoon in stock before shaping each dumpling. Continue adding dumplings until mixture is finished. Cover saucepan with a tight-fitting lid and simmer for 15–20 minutes or until dumplings are cooked. Serve dumplings in soup and garnish with remaining teaspoon of parsley.

Serves 2–3.

(per serve)
Kj—1060
Cal—253
Protein—26.7g
Fat—15.3g
Carbo—4.9g
Fibre—<1.0g

Creamy prawn bisque

PUREE

6 large prawns, cooked, shelled and deveined

2 tablespoons tomato paste

1 cup (250 ml) chicken stock

1/4 cup (60 ml) cream

pinch of paprika

pinch of pepper

1 tablespoon dry sherry (optional)

In the bowl of a food processor fitted with the steel blade or in a blender, purée prawns, tomato paste and 1/4 cup (60 ml) of chicken stock together. Scrape down sides with a spatula and process for another 30 seconds. Whilst machine is running, slowly add remaining 3/4 cup (185 ml) of stock and process to combine.

Place prawn mixture in a saucepan over low heat, stirring frequently, for about 5 minutes or until soup is hot. Stir in cream, paprika and pepper and cook for 2 minutes. Stir in sherry and serve immediately.

Serves 2.

BEATING NAUSEA

Eating fatty or fried foods can worsen feelings of nausea, so instead favour a low-fat diet abundant in starches, sugars and proteins (meat, fish and eggs) that prompt your stomach to empty more quickly. Symptoms are sometimes relieved by eating salty or sour foods like crackers, dry toast and yeast spreads, or tart foods like lemon. Flat dry ginger ale, lemonade or glucose drinks may help, particularly if vomiting is a problem.

Italian fried fish with lemon sauce

CHEWY

(per serve)
Kj—1500
Cal—358
Protein—35.0g
Fat—18.0g
Carbo—12.4g
Fibre—<1.0g

$^1/_4$ cup (30 g) plain flour
$^1/_4$ teaspoon salt
pinch of pepper
$^1/_3$ cup (30 g) dry breadcrumbs
$^1/_8$ teaspoon dried oregano
1 egg, lightly beaten
2 × 150 g firm white fish fillets (e.g. ling or sea perch)
1 tablespoon vegetable oil
2 teaspoons butter
2 teaspoons fresh lemon juice

On a flat plate mix flour, salt and pepper together. On another flat plate, mix breadcrumbs and oregano together.

Dip fish fillets into flour, shake off excess, then dip into beaten egg and finally breadcrumbs.

Heat oil in a non-stick frying pan over medium heat and fry fish for about 4–6 minutes or until golden brown on both sides and cooked through. Remove from pan, set aside and keep warm.

In the same pan, melt butter and stir in lemon juice. Spoon sauce over fish and serve immediately.

Serves 2.

Sweet potato and pumpkin casserole

SOFT MOVING

(per serve)
Kj—2120
Cal—506
Protein—28.0g
Fat—28.4g
Carbo—34.0g
Fibre—2.7g

1 medium sweet potato (about 95 g), peeled and cut into 1 cm × 2 cm pieces
95 g butternut pumpkin, peeled and cut into 1 cm × 2 cm pieces
1 teaspoon olive oil
2 eggs, lightly beaten
1 cup (250 ml) milk
1 cup cooked macaroni
³/₄ cup (90 g) grated cheddar cheese
¹/₄ teaspoon salt
¹/₄ teaspoon pepper
¹/₄ teaspoon nutmeg

Preheat oven to 200°C. Line a baking tray with baking paper. Grease an ovenproof dish with olive oil.

In a bowl, mix sweet potato, pumpkin and oil together. Spread vegetables out on tray and bake for 20–30 minutes or until cooked, turning after 15 minutes.

In a large bowl, mix eggs, milk, macaroni, baked vegetables, ¹/₂ cup of the cheese, salt, pepper and nutmeg together. Spoon mixture into prepared dish and sprinkle with remaining ¹/₄ cup of cheddar cheese. Bake casserole for 20–25 minutes or until top is golden brown.

Serves 2–3.

(per serve)
Kj—1310
Cal—313
Protein—15.0g
Fat—10.3g
Carbo—36.5g
Fibre—6.7g

Creamed corn on toast

SOFT

1 × 125 g can creamed corn
1 egg, lightly beaten
pepper to taste
1 slice thick wholemeal bread
smear of butter

In a small non-stick saucepan, heat corn for about 2 minutes or until hot. Add egg with a wooden spoon and stir constantly until corn has thickened and egg is cooked. Add pepper to taste.

Toast bread until light brown. Spread with a smear of butter. Top with hot creamed corn and serve immediately.

Makes 1 serve.

(per serve)
Kj—465
Cal—111
Protein—3.0g
Fat—3.2g
Carbo—16.2g
Fibre—2.0g

Buttered potatoes

SOFT SOOTHING and CALMING

2 medium Desiree potatoes, peeled and cut into chunks
pinch of salt
2 teaspoons butter
1/2 teaspoon chopped parsley

In a saucepan of boiling salted water, boil potatoes for 15–20 minutes or until they are soft, but not falling apart. Drain all water from potatoes and return to stove. Place a tight-fitting lid on the saucepan and, over medium heat, shake saucepan for 1 minute. Add butter and salt, replace lid and continue shaking the saucepan over the heat for 1 minute. The potatoes should have broken up. Garnish with parsley and serve.

Serves 1–2.

Vegetable biriyani

CHEWY MOVING

(per serve)
Kj—1525
Cal—364
Protein—10.2g
Fat—8.8g
Carbo—58.5g
Fibre—3.7g

2 teaspoons butter

$^1/_4$ teaspoon turmeric

$^1/_4$ teaspoon cinnamon

pinch of nutmeg

$^1/_8$ teaspoon ground coriander

pinch of chilli powder (optional)

$^1/_2$ cup (100 g) basmati or long-grain rice

1 cup (250 ml) hot vegetable stock

$^1/_4$ cup (50 g) frozen peas, thawed and blanched in boiling water for 1 minute

$^1/_2$ carrot, peeled, diced and steamed for 5 minutes

$^1/_4$ cup (30 g) canned corn kernels, drained

2 tablespoons chopped toasted cashew nuts

1 tablespoon sultanas

$^1/_4$ teaspoon salt

plain acidophilus yoghurt for serving

In a medium non-stick saucepan, heat butter over medium heat and sauté turmeric, cinnamon, nutmeg, coriander and chilli for 30 seconds. Add rice and cook for 3 minutes, stirring constantly. Add stock and bring to the boil, stirring constantly. Reduce heat, cover with a tight-fitting lid and simmer for about 15 minutes until stock is absorbed and rice is tender.

Turn off heat and fold in vegetables, cashews, sultanas and salt. Return lid to saucepan so that the vegetables warm up. Serve rice hot with yoghurt.

Serves 1–2.

TIP *This is a tasty Indian dish, full of flavour and texture. It is good to reheat in the microwave oven the next day.*

(per serve)
Kj—1935
Cal—462
Protein—19.5g
Fat—9.8g
Carbo—67.3g
Fibre—10.4g

Creamy vegetable stroganoff

SOFT

1 teaspoon olive oil

1/2 small onion, diced

1 clove garlic, crushed

1 small carrot, peeled and diced

1 small potato, peeled and diced

1 tablespoon tomato paste

3/4 cup (185 ml) vegetable stock

8 small white mushrooms, cut in half

1 cup (180 g) broccoli florets

1 teaspoon cornflour

2 tablespoons plain acidophilus yoghurt

2 tablespoons sour cream

200 g dry egg noodles

In a medium saucepan, heat oil and sauté onion for about 3 minutes or until golden. Add garlic and sauté for 30 seconds. Add carrot, potato, tomato paste and stock. Bring to the boil, stirring occasionally. Reduce heat to simmer for 10 minutes. Add mushrooms and broccoli and cook for 5 minutes. Turn off heat.

In a small saucepan, mix cornflour, yoghurt and sour cream together. Heat gently over low heat for 1 minute, stirring constantly with a wooden spoon. Add sour cream mixture to vegetables and stir well.

Meanwhile, in a saucepan of boiling salted water, cook noodles for 6–8 minutes or until tender. Drain well. Top with vegetable stroganoff and serve.

Serves 2.

Broccoli and cheese ramekins

SOFT MOVING

(per serve)
Kj—1405
Cal—336
Protein—23.9g
Fat—21.7g
Carbo—8.7g
Fibre—5.6g

2 cups (360 g) broccoli florets

2 teaspoons olive oil

1 small onion, peeled and grated on a box grater

2 eggs, separated

1/2 cup (120 g) ricotta cheese

1 tablespoon chopped parsley

1 tablespoon chopped fresh oregano or 1 teaspoon dried oregano

2 tablespoons grated cheddar cheese

1 tablespoon grated parmesan cheese

1 slice wholemeal bread, grated on a box grater

1/4 teaspoon salt

1/4 teaspoon pepper

Preheat oven to 220°C. Oil two 1-cup ramekin dishes with vegetable oil.

Steam broccoli for 5 minutes. Cool.

In a small frying pan, heat oil and sauté onion for 3 minutes or until golden brown.

In blender or food processor, purée broccoli, onion, egg yolks and ricotta together.

In a large bowl, beat egg whites until they form stiff, glossy peaks.

In a bowl, mix broccoli mixture, parsley, oregano, cheddar and parmesan cheeses, bread, salt and pepper together. Fold egg whites into broccoli mixture. Pour mixture evenly into prepared ramekin dishes. Tap the bottom of each dish lightly on the kitchen bench to break any air bubbles and smooth the top of the ramekins with a spatula. Place the ramekins on a baking tray in the oven. Turn oven down to 190°C and bake for about 25–30 minutes or until they are puffed and golden brown. Serve immediately.

Serves 2.

(per serve)
Kj—1855
Cal—443
Protein—24.2g
Fat—34.4g
Carbo—8.2g
Fibre—4.2g

Asparagus and sun-dried tomato frittata

FIRM and CHEWY

8 spears asparagus, cut into 2.5 cm lengths
1 tablespoon olive oil
1 medium leek, thinly sliced
3 eggs, lightly beaten
2 tablespoons milk
1/2 cup (60 g) grated cheddar cheese
1 tablespoon grated parmesan cheese
3 sun-dried tomatoes, preserved in oil, drained and chopped
pinch of salt
pinch of pepper
2 teaspoons olive oil

Steam asparagus for 3 minutes or until it is crisp and tender.

In a medium non-stick frying pan, over medium heat, heat 1 tablespoon oil and sauté leek for 3 minutes or until it is wilted.

In a bowl, combine eggs, asparagus, leek, milk, cheeses, tomatoes, salt and pepper.

In the same frying pan, over high heat, heat 1 teaspoon oil. Pour in egg mixture and cook, stirring or swirling the surface of the mixture with the back of a fork. Cover with a lid, reduce heat to medium–low and cook for 5 minutes or until frittata begins to brown on the bottom. Remove frittata from pan and put on to a plate. Heat remaining 1 teaspoon oil in the same pan over medium heat. Return frittata to pan by inverting plate over pan, so frittata is brown side up, and cook for another 2 minutes. Serve frittata either hot or at room temperature.

Serves 2–3.

Chinese braised cauliflower

SOFT MOVING

(per serve)
Kj—1170
Cal—280
Protein—7.8g
Fat—3.2g
Carbo—52.5g
Fibre—3.0g

1 teaspoon olive oil

1 clove garlic, crushed

1 teaspoon grated fresh ginger

2 cups (360 g) cauliflower florets

2 teaspoons soy sauce

1 teaspoon vegetarian oyster sauce

3/4 cup (185 ml) chicken or vegetable stock

2 teaspoons cornflour

3 teaspoons water

2 cups (370 g) hot cooked rice

Heat oil in a wok or non-stick frying pan and stir-fry garlic and ginger for 30 seconds. Add cauliflower and stir-fry for about 3 minutes. Add soy sauce, oyster sauce and stock and cover with a lid. Cook over medium heat for 8–10 minutes or until cauliflower is tender.

In a small bowl, mix cornflour and water together. Add cornflour mixture to wok and stir until mixture boils and thickens slightly. Serve braised cauliflower on hot rice.

Serves 2.

MEDICATION MAYHEM

Medication can affect appetite and taste, and cause nausea. A metallic taste is sometimes a side effect of vitamin deficiencies and can accompany some cancer treatments. Dental gels and throat sprays can also anaesthetise the throat and change our perceptions of taste.

Mushrooms in tomato sauce with spaghetti

FIRM and CHEWY

1 tablespoon olive oil

1 small onion, *diced*

1 clove garlic, *crushed (optional)*

12 medium white mushrooms, *sliced*

1 × 400 g can chopped tomatoes in tomato juice

2 tablespoons tomato paste

$^1/_2$ teaspoon dried basil

$^1/_2$ teaspoon dried oregano

$^1/_2$ teaspoon sugar *(optional)*

salt and pepper to taste

150 g dry spaghetti

1 tablespoon parmesan cheese

To make the sauce: in a medium saucepan, heat oil and sauté onion for about 3 minutes or until golden. Add garlic and sauté for 30 seconds. Add mushrooms and sauté for 2 minutes. Add tomatoes, juice, tomato paste, basil, oregano, sugar, salt and pepper. Bring to the boil, stirring constantly. Reduce heat and simmer for 20 minutes.

Meanwhile, in another saucepan of boiling salted water, cook pasta for about 6–8 minutes or until tender. Drain well. Serve pasta topped with mushroom sauce and cheese.

Serves 2.

OVER CATER
Preparing meals in bulk will save you time and trouble, and you'll be especially glad of your preparedness on those days when you are not feeling at your best. Most foods will keep well in the refrigerator for 2–3 days. For longer storage, pop dishes in the freezer.

Eggplant and garlic dip

SOFT MOVING

(per serve)
Kj—155
Cal—37
Protein—<1.0g
Fat—3.1g
Carbo—1.1g
Fibre—1.0g

1 medium eggplant

1 tablespoon olive oil

1/4–1/2 clove garlic, minced

1/2 teaspoon ground cumin

1 tablespoon fresh lemon juice

pinch of cayenne pepper (optional)

salt to taste

1 tablespoon chopped parsley

dry crackers for serving

Preheat a charcoal griller or grill. Grill eggplant for 25–30 minutes, turning every 10 minutes, until char-grilled. Cool and remove skin, squeeze out excess juice.

In a bowl, mash eggplant with a fork. Add oil, garlic, cumin, cayenne pepper, salt and parsley. Serve warm or cold with dry crackers. Remaining dip can be stored in an airtight container in the refrigerator for up to 3 days.

Makes 1 cup (250 ml).

TIP *Raw garlic is used in this recipe; the longer the dip is kept the stronger the garlic flavour and spiciness becomes.*

14

desserts & sweet delights

Recipe	Texture	Effect on Symptom	Type	Page
Banana rice pudding				
	SOFT	MOVING and CALMING	D, G	124
Apricot sago with vanilla yoghurt				
	SOFT	MOVING and SOOTHING	D, G	125
Fruity cheese-filled rockmelon				
	CHEWY	MOVING	G	126
Frozen strawberry and yoghurt cups				
	SOFT	SOOTHING	G	126
Blackberry bread and butter custard				
	SOFT		D	127
Apple and strawberry custard crumble				
	SOFT and CRUNCHY			128
Sticky date muffins with custard				
	CHEWY	MOVING		129
Stewed fruit with cashew date cream				
	SOFT	MOVING	G, L	130
Warm chocolate pudding				
	SOFT			131
Rhubarb fool				
	PUREE	MOVING	G	132
Vanilla junket				
	PUREE		D, G	132
Fruit trifle				
	SOFT			133
Banana and apricot custard				
	SOFT and CHEWY			134
Strawberry flummery				
	SOFT	SOOTHING	D, G	134
Chocolate mousse				
	PUREE		G	135

(per serve)
Kj—1290
Cal—308
Protein—11.8g
Fat—5.1g
Carbo—52.7g
Fibre—2.6g

Banana rice pudding

SOFT MOVING and CALMING

1 cup (185 g) cooked brown rice

3/4 cup (185 ml) low-fat milk

1 egg, lightly beaten

1 ripe banana, mashed

2 teaspoons brown sugar

1 teaspoon vanilla essence

1/2 teaspoon nutmeg

Preheat oven to 160°C. Butter 2 small ovenproof dishes.

In a medium bowl, whisk rice, milk, egg, banana, sugar, vanilla essence and 1/4 teaspoon nutmeg together. Pour mixture into prepared dishes. Sprinkle remaining 1/4 teaspoon nutmeg on top of puddings.

Put dishes into a larger pan and place the pan on the middle shelf of the oven. Pour boiling water into the pan until it comes three-quarters of the way up the sides of the dishes. Bake puddings for 30–35 minutes or until golden brown and firm. Carefully remove the dishes from the larger pan and let the pudding stand for 2 minutes before serving.

Serves 2.

TIP *Puddings can be covered with plastic wrap and refrigerated for up to 2 days. To reheat, place pudding in microwave oven on high for 1 minute or until warm through.*

Apricot sago with vanilla yoghurt

SOFT MOVING and SOOTHING

2 tablespoons sago
1¹/₄ cups (310 ml) apricot nectar
¹/₃ cup (50 g) chopped dried apricots
pinch of cinnamon
vanilla acidophilus yoghurt for serving

In a medium saucepan, soak sago in 1 cup of apricot nectar for 1 hour.

Meanwhile, soak apricots in remaining ¹/₄ cup (60 ml) apricot nectar for ¹/₂ hour. To sago mixture add apricots and cinnamon and stir well. Cook the sago mixture over a low heat, stirring occasionally for about 15–20 minutes or until sago is soft. Serve warm or cold with yoghurt.

Serves 2–3.

TIP *Apricot sago can be covered and refrigerated for up to 3 days and reheated in the microwave oven for 1 minute on high, stirring after 30 seconds.*

(per serve)
Kj—945
Cal—226
Protein—6.7g
Fat—3.8g
Carbo—38.2g
Fibre—2.2g

(per serve)
Kj—1020
Cal—244
Protein—11.7g
Fat—2.5g
Carbo—42.0g
Fibre—5.2g

Fruity cheese-filled rockmelon

CHEWY MOVING

1 small ripe rockmelon, peeled, cut in half and seeded
1/2 cup (120 g) cottage cheese
1/4 cup (50 g) chopped raisins
1/4 cup (50 g) chopped dried apricots or dried peaches
1/2 teaspoon grated orange rind
2 teaspoons honey

Place rockmelon halves onto serving plates.

In a bowl, mix cheese, raisins, apricots and orange rind together. Spoon the mixture into the rockmelon halves. Top with a drizzle of honey and serve.

Serves 2.

(per serve)
Kj—1150
Cal—275
Protein—12.2g
Fat—7.0g
Carbo—37.6g
Fibre—3.6g

Frozen strawberry and yoghurt cups

SOFT SOOTHING

8 ripe medium strawberries, washed, dried and hulled
200 ml plain acidophilus yoghurt
1 tablespoon runny honey

Line 4 muffin cases with patty papers.

Roughly chop 6 strawberries and cut the others in quarters.

In a bowl, mix yoghurt and honey together. Fold in chopped strawberries. Spoon fruit mixture into prepared pans. Top with strawberry quarters. Cover pan with plastic wrap and freeze for at least 3 hours. Allow frozen cups to soften in refrigerator for 30–40 minutes before serving.

Serves 4.

TIP *This recipe can be doubled. You can individually wrap cups in plastic wrap and keep frozen for up to 1 month. For variety, use 1 ripe chopped mango and mango yoghurt.*

Blackberry bread and butter custard

SOFT

(per serve)
Kj—1195
Cal—285
Protein—13.3g
Fat—11.5g
Carbo—32.1g
Fibre—1.1g

2 slices of white bread or fruit bread, buttered and crusts removed

2 teaspoons all-fruit blackberry jam

1 tablespoon sultanas

2 teaspoons brown sugar

2 eggs, lightly beaten

3/4 cup (185 ml) milk

1/2 teaspoon vanilla essence

Preheat oven to 180°C. Butter 2 × 1-cup ramekin dishes.

Spread jam onto bread. Cut bread to fit the ramekin dishes. Sprinkle bread with sultanas and sugar.

In a medium bowl, whisk eggs, milk and vanilla essence together. Pour milk mixture over bread. Let stand for 30 minutes. Bake for about 30 minutes or until custard is set and fluffy. Let stand for 10 minutes before serving and serve warm.

Serves 2.

TIP *For variety, use different fruit jams in the bread and butter custard.*

Recipe	Texture	Effect on Symptom	Type	Page
Fruit yoghurt jelly	PUREE	SOOTHING and CALMING	D, G	138
Home-made peanut butter	SOFT		G, L	138
Prune and apple muffins	CHEWY	MOVING		139
Chocolate buttermilk muffins	CHEWY			140
Muesli and fruit bars	CHEWY	MOVING		141
Apple and spice muffins	CHEWY	MOVING	D	142
Currant biscuits	CRUNCHY	MOVING	L	143
Gluten-free banana cake	SOFT	SOOTHING and CALMING	G	144
Walnut macaroons	CHEWY	MOVING	G, L	145
Honey Weet-Bix	PUREE	SOOTHING and MOVING		145

(per serve)
Kj—250
Cal—60
Protein—4.5g
Fat—1.1g
Carbo—7.7g
Fibre—Neg

Fruit yoghurt jelly

PUREE   SOOTHING and CALMING

1 sachet (4.5 g) low-kilojoule raspberry-flavoured jelly crystals
1 cup boiling water
¹/₂ cup (125 ml) cold water
¹/₂ cup (125 ml) fruit-flavoured acidophilus yoghurt

In a large bowl, mix jelly crystals with boiling water until crystals dissolve. Add cold water and cool jelly to room temperature. Refrigerate jelly for 20 minutes or until it is cold. Mix in yoghurt and pour into 2 glass dessert dishes. Refrigerate for 2 hours at least (or up to 2 days). Serve cold.

Serves 2.

(per serve)
Kj—800
Cal—191
Protein—7.2g
Fat—12.6g
Carbo—3.1g
Fibre—2.5g

Home-made peanut butter

SOFT

1¹/₂ cups (180 g) shelled roasted peanuts
¹/₄ teaspoon salt (optional)
¹/₂ teaspoon castor sugar (optional)

In a food processor or blender fitted with a steel blade , process peanuts for 2 minutes. The ground nuts will form a ball that gradually smoothes out. Scrape down sides with a spatula and process for a further 2 minutes for crunchy and 3–4 minutes for smooth peanut butter, or until drops of nut oil are visible. Add salt and sugar and process for 15 seconds. Place peanut butter in a sterilised airtight container and refrigerate for up to 2 weeks.

Makes ³/₄–1 cup (185–250 ml) peanut butter.

TIPS *Vary the flavour of peanut butter by adding 2 teaspoons of honey or all-fruit jam and mix well or use ¹/₂ teaspoon cinnamon as a delicious spice.*

For crunchy peanut butter, add an additional ¹/₄ cup (30 g) peanuts when you add the salt and sugar.

Prune and apple muffins

CHEWY MOVING

(per muffin)
Kj—455
Cal—109
Protein—2.5g
Fat—3.8g
Carbo—15.4g
Fibre—1.0g

8 large prunes, pitted

1/2 cup (125 ml) boiling water

2 tablespoons commercial, smooth apple sauce

1 cup (125 g) plain flour

2 teaspoons baking powder

1/4 teaspoon cinnamon

2 tablespoons castor sugar

2 tablespoons skim milk powder

3 tablespoons milk

1 egg, well beaten

2 tablespoons canola oil

Preheat oven to 200°C. Spray 2 × 6 large-cup muffin tins or 2 × 12 mini-cup muffin tins with canola oil spray or line with patty papers.

Soak prunes in boiling water for 30 minutes. Purée the prune mixture in a blender or food processor fitted with the metal blade until smooth. Add apple sauce and mix well.

In a large bowl, sift plain flour, baking powder and cinnamon together. Mix in sugar and milk powder.

In a small bowl, mix together milk, egg, oil and prune mixture. Mix this into flour mixture. Place spoonfuls of mixture into muffin tins.

Bake muffins for 15–20 minutes for large muffins or 10 minutes for mini muffins or until well risen and golden brown. Cool muffins on a wire rack. Store in an airtight container.

Makes 12 large or 24 mini muffins.

TIPS *Muffins can be individually wrapped in plastic wrap and frozen, then defrosted as needed. Muffins keep for up to 1 month in the freezer.*

For extra nutrition, add 2 tablespoons of vanilla supplement powder to milk powder.

Recipe	Texture	Effect on Symptom	Type	Page
Tropical smoothie				
	PUREE	MOVING	D, G, L	148
Peach and banana smoothie				
	PUREE	SOOTHING	D, G, L	148
Flaming red energy juice				
	PUREE	MOVING	D, G, L	148
Sports drink				
	PUREE	CALMING	G, L	149
Lite orange drink				
	PUREE			149
Pina colada smoothie				
	PUREE		G, L	149
Iced coffee				
	PUREE		D	150
Green tea sorbet				
	PUREE	SOOTHING and CALMING	G, L	150
Chai				
	PUREE		L	151
Apricot whip				
	PUREE	SOOTHING and CALMING	D, G	151

Tropical smoothie

PUREE   MOVING

1 cup (250 ml) unsweetened pineapple juice
¹/₂ ripe mango (about 125 g), peeled, stoned and cubed
¹/₂ ripe banana, peeled and chopped
ice cubes

Combine pineapple juice, mango and banana in a blender or food processor fitted with the metal blade. Process for about 1 minute or until smooth. Place ice cubes in a glass and pour smoothie over. Serve immediately.

Makes 1 serve.

Peach and banana smoothie

PUREE   SOOTHING

2 red-skinned apples, washed, cored and roughly chopped
1 ripe peach, washed, stoned and roughly chopped
2 frozen bananas, peeled and roughly chopped

In a juice extractor, juice apples and peach.

Combine juice and bananas in a blender or food processor fitted with a metal blade. Process for about 1 minute or until smooth. Serve immediately.

Makes 1 serve.

Flaming red energy juice

PUREE   MOVING

1 small red-skinned apple, washed, cored and roughly chopped
6 spinach leaves, washed
2 lettuce leaves, washed
¹/₂ small beetroot, washed and roughly chopped
2 sprigs parsley
1 stick celery, washed and roughly chopped

In a juice extractor, juice apple, spinach, lettuce, beetroot, parsley and celery. Pour into a glass and serve immediately.

Makes 1 serve.

Sports drink

PUREE CALMING

2 tablespoons sugar
$^1/_8$ teaspoon salt
3 cups (750 ml) hot caffeine-free lemon and ginger tea
$^1/_4$ cup (60 ml) fresh apple juice

Dissolve sugar and salt in the hot tea. Mix in apple juice. Refrigerate drink until it is cold.

Makes $3^1/_2$ cups (810 ml).

🍎 **TIP** *For variety, use different flavoured caffeine-free teas and orange juice.*

Lite orange drink

PUREE

2 tablespoons runny honey
2 cups (500 ml) cold water
1 cup (250 ml) fresh orange juice
2 tablespoons fresh lemon juice
thin slices of orange
ice cubes

In a large clean jar or pitcher, dissolve honey in water. Mix in orange and lemon juices. Cover and refrigerate for up to 2 days. When serving add slices of orange and a few ice cubes to a tall glass, pour in orange drink and serve.

Makes about 3 cups (750 ml).

Pina colada smoothie

PUREE

$^1/_2$ cup (125 ml) unsweetened pineapple juice
$^1/_4$ cup (50 g) pineapple pieces, drained
$^1/_2$ cup (125 ml) coconut milk

Combine pineapple juice, pineapple pieces and coconut milk in a blender or food processor fitted with a metal blade. Process for about 1 minute or until smooth. Strain the smoothie through a strainer for a smoother texture. Serve immediately.

Makes 1 serve.

(per serve)
Kj—950
Cal—227
Protein—9.4g
Fat—11.6g
Carbo—22.5g
Fibre—Neg

Iced coffee

PUREE

1 teaspoon instant coffee
1 teaspoon boiling water
1/2 cup (125 ml) milk
1 tablespoon skim milk powder
1/2 cup (125 ml) vanilla ice-cream
ice cubes

Dissolve coffee in water and put into a blender or bowl of a food processor fitted with a metal blade. Add milk, milk powder and ice-cream and blend for about 1 minute or until smooth. Serve over ice cubes in a tall glass.

Makes 1 serve.

TIP *For added nutrition, add 2 tablespoons of supplement powder and stir well.*

(per cup)
Kj—620
Cal—148
Protein—Neg
Fat—Neg
Carbo—39.0g
Fibre—Neg

Green tea sorbet

PUREE   SOOTHING and CALMING

8 green tea teabags
2 cups (500 ml) boiling water
2 cups (500 ml) water
3/4 cup (180 g) castor sugar
3 tablespoons lemon juice

In a heatproof jug, steep tea bags in boiling water for 5 minutes. Remove tea bags and squeeze dry.

In a medium saucepan, bring additional water and sugar to a boil and boil for 2 minutes. Remove from the heat and add tea and lemon juice. Pour mixture into a clean jug and refrigerate for 2 hours or until cold.

Place mixture in an ice-cream maker and process until mixture forms a sorbet. Remove from the ice-cream maker, place in a container and freeze.

Makes 4 cups (1 litre).

Chai

PUREE

In many parts of the world, tea is called 'chai'. This fragrant tea can be served hot or ice cold.

(per cup)
Kj—905
Cal—217
Protein—4.1g
Fat—3.5g
Carbo—41.2g
Fibre—<1.0g

2 cups (500 ml) rice milk or vanilla-flavoured rice milk
2 cups (500 ml) water
2 tablespoons black tea leaves (Assam or breakfast)
¹/₂ cup (125 g) castor sugar
1 × 6 cm stick cinnamon
6 whole peppercorns
pinch of ground cloves
¹/₈ teaspoon nutmeg
¹/₈ teaspoon ground ginger

In a medium saucepan, heat rice milk, water, tea leaves and sugar until mixture boils. Remove from heat and add cinnamon, peppercorns, cloves, nutmeg and ginger. Cover saucepan with a lid and leave for 15 minutes while the flavours develop. Remove lid and reheat mixture until it boils. Remove from heat and strain through a fine, heat-resistant strainer into cups, teapot or a clean glass jar, or refrigerate until cold. The chai can be stored in the refrigerator for up to 2 days.

Makes about 4 cups (1 litre).

Apricot whip

PUREE SOOTHING and CALMING

(per serve)
Kj—740
Cal—177
Protein—8.1g
Fat—<1.0g
Carbo—33.6g
Fibre—1.5g

³/₄ cup (185 ml) apricot nectar
¹/₂ ripe banana, peeled and roughly chopped
2 tablespoons skim milk powder
1 teaspoon fresh lemon juice
ice cubes

In a blender or bowl of a food processor fitted with a metal blade, blend apricot nectar, banana, milk powder and lemon juice for about 1 minute or until smooth. Serve over ice cubes in a tall glass.

Makes 1 serve.

17

nutritional supplements

Strawberry shake

PUREE

(per serve)
Kj—1480
Cal—354
Protein—14.3g
Fat—19.7g
Carbo—31.4g
Fibre—<1.0g

1/2 cup (125 ml) strawberry-flavoured supplement powder
3/4 cup (185 ml) milk or water
1/2 cup (125 ml) strawberry ice-cream
3 ripe strawberries, washed, hulled and roughly chopped

In a blender or food processor fitted with a metal blade, blend powder, milk or water, ice-cream and strawberries together until smooth, about 2 minutes. Pour shake into a glass and serve.

Makes 1 serve.

TIP *Add fresh banana, mango or peach for variety.*

Iced mocha coffee

PUREE

(per serve)
Kj—1450
Cal—346
Protein—15.6g
Fat—12.2g
Carbo—45.9g
Fibre—Neg

1 teaspoon instant coffee
1 teaspoon boiling water
1/2 cup (125 ml) milk
1 tablespoon skim milk powder
2 tablespoons vanilla- or chocolate-flavoured supplement powder
1 tablespoon chocolate syrup (optional)
1/2 cup (125 ml) vanilla, coffee or chocolate ice-cream

Dissolve coffee in water. In a blender or food processor fitted with a metal blade, blend coffee, milk, milk powder, supplement powder, chocolate syrup and ice-cream for about 1 minute or until smooth. Serve immediately in a tall glass.

Makes 1 serve.

Albion Street home-made supplement drink

PUREE

(per serve)
Kj—515
Cal—123
Protein—8.4g
Fat—2.5g
Carbo—17.0g
Fibre—Neg

1 kg milk powder or skim milk powder

1 cup (250 g) sugar

1 cup (100 g) chocolate drink powder or 2 teaspoons vanilla essence when adding water

Mix together and store in an airtight container. To make up, mix $^1/_4$–$^1/_3$ cup of powder with 1 cup cold water and stir.

Strawberries and banana with vanilla custard

SOFT

(per serve)
Kj—1610
Cal—385
Protein—15.0g
Fat—8.3g
Carbo—62.6g
Fibre—3.2g

6 ripe strawberries, washed, hulled and chopped

1 ripe banana, roughly chopped

1 tablespoon custard powder

2 heaped tablespoons vanilla-flavoured supplement powder

2 teaspoons castor sugar

$^3/_4$ cup (185 ml) milk

Place strawberries and banana in dessert bowl or bowls.

In a small saucepan, combine custard powder, supplement powder and sugar with a little of the milk, to form a paste. Add remaining milk and heat, stirring constantly with a wooden spoon, until custard thickens and just boils. Reduce heat and simmer for 1 minute, stirring constantly. Either cool custard to room temperature or serve warm. Pour the custard over fruit and serve.

Serves 1–2.

(per muffin)
Kj—710
Cal—170
Protein—6.0g
Fat—5.6g
Carbo—22.1g
Fibre—3.4g

Peach and almond muffins

CHEWY MOVING

1¹/₂ cups (190 g) plain wholemeal flour

1¹/₂ teaspoons baking powder

¹/₂ teaspoon cinnamon

¹/₄ teaspoon mixed spice (optional)

3 heaped tablespoons vanilla-flavoured supplement powder

¹/₄ cup (30 g) finely chopped almonds

1 egg, well beaten

¹/₂ cup (125 ml) unsweetened apple juice

1 tablespoon olive oil

¹/₂ cup (100 g) canned peaches in natural juice, drained and finely chopped

Preheat oven to 200°C. Spray 2 × 6 large-cup muffin tins or 2 × 12 mini-cup muffin tins with canola oil spray or line with patty papers.

In a large bowl, sift wholemeal flour, baking powder, cinnamon and mixed spice, add bits from the sifter to the flour. Mix in supplement powder and almonds.

In a small bowl, mix egg, apple juice, oil and peaches together. Mix milk mixture into flour mixture. Place spoonfuls of mixture in muffin tins.

Bake muffins for 15–20 minutes for large muffins or 10 minutes for mini muffins or until well risen and golden brown. Cool muffins on a wire rack. Store in an airtight container.

Makes 8 large or 16 mini muffins.

GO NUTTY

Nuts and seeds are high in fibre and make a good high-energy snack. Pumpkin, sunflower or sesame seeds are a delicious addition to cereals and salads.

Resources

Contact details for the state-based groups are listed on the websites below, or can be found by telephoning or writing to the federal organisation.

Aged Care
Commonwealth Department of Aged and Community Care
Freecall 1800 500 853
Website: www.health.gov.au/acc

Diabetes
Diabetes Australia
1st floor, Churchill House
218 Northbourne Avenue, Braddon ACT 2612
Freecall: 1300 136 588
Website: www.diabetesaustralia.com.au

Eating Disorders
ACT: Women's Centre for Health Matters
Building One, Pearce Centre
Collett Place, Pearce ACT 2607
Ph: (02) 6290 2166

NSW: Eating Disorder Support Network
PO Box 532, Willoughby NSW 2068
Ph: (02) 9412 4499
Website: www.edsn.asn.au

NSW: Eating Disorders Association of NSW Inc.
PO Box 811
Castle Hill NSW 2154
Ph: (02) 9899 5344 Fax: (02) 9899 5811
Website: www.edansw.org.au

QLD: Eating Disorders Resource Centre
53 Railway Terrace, Milton QLD 4064
Ph: (07) 3876 2500 Fax: (07) 3511 6959
Website: www.uq.net.au/eda/

SA: Eating Disorders Association of South Australia Inc.
Woodards House
2nd Floor, 47–49 Waymouth Street
Adelaide SA 5000
Ph: (08) 8212 1644 Fax: (08) 8212 7991

TAS: Community Nutrition Unit
3rd Floor, Peacock Building
Repatriation Centre, Hampden Road
Battery Point TAS 7004
Ph: (03) 6222 7222 Fax: (03) 6222 7252

VIC: Eating Disorders Foundation of Victoria
1513 High Street, Glen Iris VIC 3146
Ph: (03) 9885 0318 Fax: (03) 9855 1153
Website: www.eatingdisorders.org.au

WA: Eating Disorders Association of WA Inc.
PO Box 8015, Perth Business Centre
Perth WA 6849
Ph: (08) 9221 0488 Fax: (08) 9221 0499

HIV/AIDS
Albion Street Centre
150–154 Albion Street, Surry Hills NSW 2010
Freecall 1800 451 600
Ph: (02) 9332 1090 Fax: (02) 9331 3490
Website: www.sesahs.nsw.gov.au/albionstcentre/
Email: ALBHIVInfo@sesahs.nsw.gov.au

Australian Federation of AIDS Organisations
Level 4, 74–78 Wentworth Avenue
Surry Hills NSW 2010
Ph: (02) 9281 1999 Fax: (02) 9281 1044
Website: www.afao.org.au
Email: afao@rainbow.net.au

Motor Neurone Disease (MND) and Dysphagia (swallowing difficulties)
Motor Neurone Disease Association of Australia Inc.
Box 23, Canterbury VIC 3126
Freecall: 1800 806 632
Ph: (03) 9830 2122 Fax: (03) 9830 2228
Website: home.vicnet.net.au/~mndaust/
Email: mndvic@vicnet.net.au

The *NSW Dysphagia Resource Manual* is available from:
Concord Repatriation General Hospital
Hospital Road, Concord NSW 2139
Ph: (02) 9767 5000

The *Queensland Dysphagia Directory* is available from:
Allied Health Outreach Support Service
c/o Department of Allied Health, Cossart House
Private Mail Bag No. 2
Toowoomba QLD 4350
Ph: (07) 4616 6344

Parkinson's Disease
Parkinson's Australia Inc.
c/o Parkinson's NSW Inc.
Building 64, Concord Repatriation General Hospital
Hospital Road, Concord NSW 2139
Freecall: 1800 644 189
Ph: (02) 9767 7881
Website: www.parkinsons.org.au

Nutritional Supplement Companies
Abbott Australia
Captain Cook Drive, Kurnell NSW 2231
Freecall 1800 225 311
Website: www.abbottlabs.com.au

Novartis Australia
Website: www.novartis.com

Nutricia Australia Pty Ltd
14-16 Brookhollow Avenue, Baulkham Hills NSW 2153
Freecall 1800 060 051

General index

Recipe index